TIGER-NANNY

URSULA MORAY WILLIAMS

Tiger-nanny

Illustrated by
Gunvor Edwards

HODDER AND STOUGHTON
LONDON SYDNEY AUCKLAND TORONTO

To Eileen and Vera

ISBN 0–340–16872–2

First published 1973 by Brockhampton Press Ltd
(now Hodder and Stoughton Children's Books)
Second impression 1987

Published by Hodder and Stoughton Children's Books,
a division of Hodder and Stoughton Ltd,
Mill Road, Dunton Green, Sevenoaks, Kent TN13 2YJ

Printed in Great Britain by T. J. Press (Padstow) Ltd,
Padstow, Cornwall

Contents

1 · To be a tiger-nanny

There was a tiger cub who wanted more than anything else on earth to take care of little children.

She was born in the Zoological Gardens, and she lived in the Pets' Corner where It was soon apparent how gentle and yet firm she was with the youngest visitors. She could soothe a crying child or quell a spoilt one, resist teasing without a mite of malice, and persuade the wildest little boys to pick up their toffee papers and blow their noses.

She was the favourite of the gardens, but little tigers grow into big tigers even faster than children grow into adults, and big tigers are not popular among parents in the Pets' Corner.

'We are losing money,' the head keeper said to the director of the Zoological Gardens, 'and I think it is the tiger. People used to leave their youngest children here for a whole morning while they took the bigger ones round the zoo, but I've noticed they don't do it any longer. I can't think why. The kids are much safer with little Tig than they are in the public street.

But there you are, you can't teach people what is good for them.'

'Well, there won't be much difficulty in placing her,' said the director. 'Where shall it be? The Big Cats' House, Bellamy's Circus or a Safari Park? Ask her which she would like best.'

But the little tiger only wanted to be a children's nurse.

"Tigers can't *be* children's nurses,' the keeper explained to her.

'There was a dog once that was a children's nurse,' said the tiger cub. 'Its name was Peter Pan.'

'You've got it wrong, my dear,' said the keeper. 'Peter Pan was the little boy, not the dog. And he *never* grew up.'

'How sad,' said the tiger cub. 'He would have grown up if I had looked after him.'

'So you see, it will have to be the Big Cats' House, a Safari Park or Bellamy's Circus,' said the keeper, rubbing her ears.

'But I love little children best,' said the tiger cub.

'And if you say *that*, people think you mean – ' the keeper smacked his lips – 'yummy-yummy-yummy! See?'

'Oh!' said the tiger cub looking deeply mortified. Tears came into her gentle green eyes and she turned her head away.

'Don't take it to heart,' the keeper said kindly. 'You will see plenty of children in the Big Cats'

House or Bellamy's Circus or a Safari Park. Take your time and think it over. You can tell the director and myself at the end of the week.'

The tiger cub was still so young and so accustomed to human beings that she had plenty of freedom. But the clerk at the employment agency was very surprised when she turned up in his office on a Monday morning.

'I want to be a children's nurse,' she said.

'My dear miss or madam,' said the clerk, staring, 'I have thirty-five families on my list all asking me for children's nurses, but not one of them, not *one*, would employ a tiger.'

The tiger cub went away disappointed. The next day she was back again, much to the clerk's embarrassment.

'Now why do you think you would make a good children's nurse?' he asked her.

'I just love little children,' said the tiger cub simply.

'Ha! Parents don't like to hear that kind of talk!' said the clerk at once. He smacked his lips and leaned over his desk towards the tiger cub. '*They* think you mean – yummy-yummy-yummy!'

Deeply mortified the tiger cub left the employment agency with tears running down her chin.

The next morning, outside the employment agency but at the very end of the queue looking for other jobs, was a little old lady in a neat grey coat buttoned up to the neck. She was wearing grey woollen gloves and a felt hat pulled down to her eyebrows.

The clerk's face brightened, for here at last was the very image of the children's nurse he was looking for, and he whipped open his ledger to find one of the thirty-five addresses of families that were pestering him to supply a nanny.

'Age, madam?' he asked. 'Over fifty – under fifty? Previous experience? Any preference for first babies? How many children are you prepared to take charge of?'

'Any number,' said the little grey nurse. 'And I don't mind if they are first babies or seconds, or just little children. I love them all.'

The clerk looked up. He thought the little lady looked very hairy about the chin and her nose was a funny shape for a nanny. She also seemed rather familiar.

'Oh, it's you again!' he said slowly, as he recognized the tiger cub. 'It's no good. Nobody is going to employ you, not even in a uniform. People don't want to engage tigers to look after their children.'

'I forgot to tell you,' the tiger cub said desperately. 'I'll come for free.'

'It won't make any difference,' the clerk said. 'The higher wages people pay the better value they think they are getting. They just don't want tigers at any price.'

The tiger cub turned away looking broken-hearted.

'Wait a minute!' called the clerk. 'I'll do just one thing to help you. I don't mind putting an advertisement in the paper this evening stating the truth, the whole truth and nothing but the truth. I'll advertise a tiger wanting a post as a children's nurse, payment secondary consideration, and then perhaps you will believe what I say when I tell you that nobody will consider such a proposition for a minute.'

The next morning there was already a long queue at the employment agency when the tiger cub arrived to ask for a job. She had taken off her coat and woolly gloves but wore her hat, which she thought made her look more like a children's nanny.

The clerk did not see her at first. He was busy answering the queries of nearly forty mothers who had arrived in answer to the advertisement they had read in the evening papers. Quite contrary to the clerk's expectations every one of them seemed desperate to employ a tiger-nanny to look after their children. And most of them said they were willing to pay any wages at all to get her.

'Just a minute, just a minute, the advertiser has not yet arrived,' the clerk said, rather flustered by the urgency of the mothers crowding into his office. Then he caught sight of the tiger cub in the queue and called her to come and sit beside him. All the mothers began to talk at once. They shouted one another down, describing the charms of their families,

the claims on their time that the children made, which having a tiger-nurse would solve. Some of them wanted to play bingo, some to go abroad, some to work in offices. Some just hated looking after their own children, and others did not know how to begin to do it.

The tiger cub, sitting upright on a chair beside the clerk, looked most bewildered.

'I was quite wrong,' the clerk whispered to her. 'Everybody wants you, it seems. I am sorry, I can't do any more for you at the moment. You will have to make your own choice of a situation.'

The tiger cub was much too shy to interview the

mothers in any order of priority. She just let them shout until they were hoarse, but then suddenly she put her paws on the clerk's desk and rose to her full height, looking across their heads to the end of the queue where three children sat patiently on the edge of the pavement with their hands upon their knees.

The clamouring mothers retreated. They scattered with shrieks and screams as the tiger cub towered above them. Their retreat formed a gap the length of their ranks through which the three children could be seen sitting, patiently waiting until the hysterical grown-up clamour should die down.

They were beautiful children, quite individual,

and different from one another. And grown children they were, not toddlers, though the youngest, a boy, seemed to be about four years old. The eldest, a girl, might have been eleven. She was tall and slender with soft brown hair hanging nearly to her waist. She was beautifully dressed, but her clothes were outgrown and her dress sagged at the hem where the stitches had given way.

Her brother, a little younger than herself, was very dark, with a long proud neck like a young stag. His long hair leapt up the sides of his head and clustered at the top in a thick mop, above sharp ears. He carried himself with such dignity that no one noticed his neck was dirty – except the tiger cub, who marked it down immediately.

The youngest child was like a golden lion cub, with the smallest cluster of freckles, like stars, above his nose, at present buried in a piece of dirty blanket. Several fingers were stuffed into his mouth. His sunburned legs, like those of his brother and sister, were bare. His name was Salvatore.

'Julius!' the the tiger cub barked loudly. 'Julius! Samantha! Torie! Come here at once! I want to speak to you!'

The three children came running, and the mothers, suddenly recognizing them, began to squeak and then to whisper and finally to babble:

'They're Mandoline Harper's children!'

Mandoline Harper, on location, had been making

a film somewhere near the Zoological Gardens, directed by her latest husband, the father of Salvatore, and the children had tagged along too.

The tiger cub knew them very well, for the children had spent a great deal of their time in the Zoological Gardens, and especially in the Pets' Corner.

'Oh, so it *is* you, yourself, darling Tigs!' the children cried as they came running round the desk to hug her. 'We hoped and hoped it was you who was in the evening papers. We came to fetch you to come and be our nanny!'

The mothers re-formed their ranks and began to crowd round the desk again, protesting vigorously.

'Why, they aren't even babies! They can take care of themselves! *She* can get a nurse anywhere! Just look what she can pay them!' 'What a cheek sending the kids down here!' 'Doesn't even bother to come herself! I like her nerve!'

They began to bribe the tiger cub with the enormous wages they promised to pay her, shouting one another down as if it had been an auction sale. The clerk tried in vain to quieten them, while the tiger cub simply gathered the children round about her and set them to rights, twitching at Samantha's crooked skirt and gently removing the fingers from Salvatore's mouth.

When at last the clamour ceased for a moment everyone looked towards the clerk for his decision, while the clerk looked towards the tiger cub.

'It is for you to make up your mind,' he reminded her. One might almost think he was afraid of the persistent and predatory mothers.

'I am going to look after these children,' said the tiger cub with one paw round Julius and another round Salvatore.

There was a murmur of indignation that swelled to a shout as Samantha, Julius and their little brother prepared to leave the office.

'What about my fee?' said the clerk, putting himself immediately upon the side of the mothers.

'Don't be silly!' said Samantha, sweeping forward like a queen, with her hand on the tiger cub's little round hat. 'You know perfectly well that our mother is Mandoline Harper. Do you think *she* is going to bother about money?'

'That was very rude,' said the tiger cub, stopping short in her tracks. 'And it was very vulgar, too, to talk about money in that way. Money may take you through a turnstile but it won't make you welcome in the park. I'm not coming to you for the sake of money. I don't think I want to look after rude, vulgar little children like you.'

'Oh, Tiger-nanny! Tiger-nanny! Do come with us!' wept the three children, clinging to her neck. 'Don't you know what will happen to us if Mother can't find us a children's nurse? We're all going to be sent to boarding-school!'

'Caged up like tigers!' said Julius gloomily. 'Oh,

I beg your pardon, Tigs. I didn't mean to be rude.'

'Well, you set your sister an example there,' said the tiger-nanny. 'I'm waiting, Samantha. What do you say to the gentleman?'

'I beg your pardon!' Samantha said, turning to the clerk with a charming little curtsey. 'If you will trust us I am perfectly certain that my mother will pay you an enormous lot of money for Tiger-nanny.'

'Madam will pay the proper fee,' the tiger-nanny corrected her. 'Come along, children. Don't drag your blanket, Torie. Pick it up nicely or let me carry it for you.'

In front of all the disappointed mothers Tiger-nanny left the employment agency with two children clinging to one ear and a third to the other, carrying a dirty blanket in her mouth and looking both ways as she stepped off the pavement with her charges – in case any traffic was coming.

2 · *The children*

Mandoline Harper, star of three best-selling films and wife of three husbands, two divorced and one directing her new picture, was still in bed when her children arrived in her room with Tiger-nanny. Her secretary, who had been taking dictation from her, stepped sharply backwards into the film star's breakfast tray and sent the coffee pot flying into a pile of fan mail.

'Gently – gently!' Tiger-nanny murmured automatically. 'Pick the letters up, dear, before they get wet!' she directed Samantha.

'What on earr-rrth?' said Mandoline Harper, sitting up in bed.

'Mummy, it's our new nurse!' said little Salvatore. 'She's much better than Miss Lester, she's soft all over.'

'Well, darling-O! If you say so. I thought Daddy had sent me up a new coat!' said Mandoline, holding out her arms to her youngest. 'Come and love Mummy. Where did you get the lovely pussy from, wonder boy?'

'From the office down town,' Samantha said, taking sugar lumps from her mother's tray. 'You owe them two-fifty I believe.'

'Don't eat sugar now, dear! You'll spoil your breakfast,' said Tiger-nanny, gently removing the sugar basin. 'I hope I shall give satisfaction, madam,' she added politely.

'Mandy will be satisfied with anything that takes us off her back, won't you, Mandy?' said the boy Julius. Tiger-nanny tut-tutted as his mother's lip went down.

'Oh, Julio-angel, don't talk like that!' she said. 'You know Mamma loves having you around, she really does. It's only that she's so very, very busy from morning till night – just look at all those letters now!' and she pointed at the morning's mail, spread out by Samantha like postage stamps to dry on the silk counterpane.

'Dirty girl,' Tiger-nanny murmured and Samantha blanched.

'Tell Elwyn to send the money down to the place,' Mandoline told her daughter. The secretary had left the room. Turning on the charm that had made her famous, she added to Tiger-nanny:

'Are you really going to take charge of my poppets, you beauty-beast? Are you coming into my family? I can tell you there's a great big welcome waiting here for you if you are good to my babies.'

'Stepdad won't like it!' Julius muttered, floating

crispbread on his mother's unfinished coffee. 'He didn't like the monkey or the cheetah or the python or the –'

'Julio – don't!' said his mother plaintively. 'And don't call him Stepdad, he doesn't like it a bit. Call him Lucien if you want to, but why not just Daddy, like Torie does? And Torie can ask him about the tiger-nurse. Daddy always says yes to Torie.'

Salvatore's cub face glowed as he pushed himself and his blanket closer into his mother's pillows.

'Go and have breakfast, sweety-pop,' she said, giving him a little push, 'and *wash*, mooey-moo, wash all over!'

'I'll see to it, madam,' said Tiger-nanny.

'Kiss Fluff first!' said Salvatore, thrusting his blanket into her face. Mandoline Harper obeyed, wincing.

'I'll see to Fluff too, madam,' said Tiger-nanny, leading Salvatore from the room with the blanket held between her teeth.

'Oh, Tiger-nanny!' Mandoline called after her. 'Just a moment!'

'Yes, madam?'

'I'm sure you'll be absolutely wonderful with the kids . . .' Mandoline Harper said, lying back on her pillows. 'I can see you're a kind of a genius that way, but – er – I mean – you will just remember that human kids haven't any scruffs to their necks to pick them up by, won't you? I mean, they're not like tigers.'

Young as she was, the feelings of righteous indignation rising in her breast threatened to overwhelm Tiger-nanny's composure. But she thrust them aside.

'Yes, madam. I had noticed it,' she replied calmly.

'And if there's anything you want, ask Elwyn Bankes to get it for you. She's my secretary. She'll see to your wages too,' Mandoline Harper added, picking up the first of her fan mail envelopes and shaking it so that a little spatter of coffee drips tickled Tiger-nanny's nose.

'Thank you, madam,' said Tiger-nanny, leaving the room.

Some half an hour later, with the children washed and brushed and Salvatore's blanket drying on the window sill, Tiger-nanny faced her new responsibilities across a late breakfast table.

'We have never had a nanny for more than a week at a time,' Samantha said. 'I mean to enjoy every minute of you.'

'Then mind your manners so I can enjoy you too, dear,' said Tiger-nanny. 'Remember, there are forty more families down at the employment agency all anxious to employ me if you make my life impossible.'

'Oh *no*, Tiger-nanny! We'll be gooder than any children you ever heard of!' the children shrieked. 'We'll never, never, *never* let you go!'

At that moment the door of the nursery apartment

was flung open and in strode a short fat man so like Salvatore to look at that nobody could doubt it was his father.

'What's all this about?' he roared in a grown-up version of Salvatore's voice. Tiger-nanny almost expected to see a piece of blanket sticking out of his pocket but there was only a pale mauve silk handkerchief to match his shirt.

'Julius! Samantha! If I haven't said a dozen times that we can't carry a train of animals around with us on location! And you know perfectly well what cats do to my asthma! I should think a tiger will about finish me off. You needn't think you can get round your mother. I'm not having a tiger in the family.'

Little Salvatore immediately burst into tears and choked over his breakfast, involving his cornflakes and the front of the clean shirt Tiger-nanny had just put upon him.

'There!' she scolded. 'Little boys *do* need bibs. I told you so. I'm very sorry, sir,' she added, seeing his father's look of disgust. 'He is just a little upset. And I'll make you up some friar's balsam to inhale, sir, with a little salt and TCP. It does a world of good to asthma.'

The film director stared at her, as well he might.

'Where did you get all that from?' he asked her.

'Oh, you hear things in the gardens, sir, and I keep my ears open,' said Tiger-nanny, patting Torie on the back with one paw and fixing on a bib

with the other. 'Now then, Torie, dear, we'll start again shall we? Right paw for your spoon, unless he's left-handed. Is he left-handed?' she asked his elder brother and sister as the father left the room, muttering.

'No,' said Julius.

'Sometimes,' said Samantha.

'Well then, suppose you use whichever you can manage best with,' said Tiger-nanny. Little Salvatore at once began to eat with a spoon in each hand.

'Isn't that clever!' said Tiger-nanny admiringly.

'And I think you manage much better with the right one, don't you? So we'll let it get on all by itself.'

'Stepdad will never let you go now, Tiggo,' said Julius, lounging in his chair. 'We only have to tell Sally to cry and he gets us whatever we want. It's easy. Stepdad won't do a thing for Sam or me.'

'Well, it is hardly surprising if you don't treat him more politely,' Tiger-nanny said. 'You heard what your mother said: your stepfather doesn't like what you call him. You could begin by saying his name nicely. If you don't want to call him by his Christian name, which is quite right, and you shouldn't use your mother's either, why not "Father" or "Stepfather" or even "Sir"? Courtesy is not the privilege of kings. And I don't like to hear you give your little brother a girl's name and your sister a boy's name. My own name, by the way, is Tiger-nanny.'

'Shall you punish us, Tiger-nanny?' Samantha asked after a long pause. 'We have never been punished and it would be so exciting.'

'I shall not spank you,' said Tiger-nanny, 'if that is what you mean. My mother always said that was a mother's privilege. And I can't see what is so exciting about being sent to bed on bread and water.'

'Currant bread would be!' said Samantha. 'I adore currant bread. And just a little orange in the water, or some wine. And I love going to bed. There never seems to be enough time for it on location.'

'I shall have to get a book on child care and look up some more punishments,' said Tiger-nanny.

'Ooh, yes, do let's!' said Samantha, Julius and Salvatore.

3 · *Prisoner in the zoo*

Some half hour later Mandoline Harper was leaving her apartment to join the film set, accompanied by her husband.

Tiger-nanny was waiting in the vestibule.

'If you please, madam, would it inconvenience you if I had an hour off this afternoon, just to tell my family that I have found a situation? I thought if I went while the children have their rests Miss Bankes would keep an eye on them till I get back.'

'Their *rests*?' their mother said blankly.

'Excellent, excellent. Keep them off the set at any price,' said Lucien, her husband.

'Well of course you can go, Nanny!' said Mandoline, greatly relieved. She was afraid that the director might have made a scene. 'I've told Miss Bankes to pay the money to the bureau!' she called back over her shoulder, stepping into the car.

'But we don't rest, we aren't *babies*!' Julius expostulated when lunch was over and Tiger-nanny put on her little felt hat. 'You look silly in that hat,' he added unkindly.

'Little boys who are young enough to be rude are young enough to rest in the afternoon,' Tiger-nanny replied tartly. 'Get something to read and lie on your beds. Salvatore is fast asleep already.'

'I love resting!' came Samantha's joyful voice from her mother's bedroom. 'I've borrowed Mandy's new negligee and I'm reading the book Lucien keeps under his shirts in the dressing-room.'

'Samantha!' said Tiger-nanny severely. 'Take off your mother's dressing-gown, and put that book back where you found it. There are some nice Enid Blytons on the shelves and your own wrap is hanging on the door.'

'Do come back soon, Tiger-nanny!' said the secretary, peering anxiously round the door. 'I can't do a thing with them, and little Torie always wakes up in a screaming rage. You won't be long, will you?'

'I shan't be more than an hour,' Tiger-nanny promised. 'Now be good, you three!' she called loudly. 'If there's any trouble I shall hear all about it from Miss Bankes.'

'We'll be good!' shouted Julius and Samantha. Little Salvatore was sleeping soundly. Tiger-nanny put his blanket (now dry and smelling of Lux) beside him on the pillow and crept out of the door.

She was quite overwhelmed by the fuss and commotion that met her at the Zoological Gardens. The morning had been so occupied that she had not had time to think that she might be missed. She had never been away so long before.

The Pets' Corner was in a frenzy, with everyone searching for her. All the keepers were rushing about and telephoning. Her loss had just been reported on the BBC midday news.

The keeper who met her trotting up the path to the Big Cats' House bundled her into his arms and carried her straight to her mother, where the big tigers bowled her over and bit and scolded her, so that Tiger-nanny hardly noticed the door of the cage had been closed and the bolt shot home.

'Where have you *been*?' her mother kept saying over and over again. Tiger-nanny, who thought she had quite outgrown her mother's affections, was very bewildered. She explained about her situation and was pleased to find that her mother was at least impressed.

But it appeared that she should never, *never* have gone off like that and fixed herself up with a situation without first asking permission from the head keeper or the director of the Zoological Gardens.

This seemed very unreasonable to Tiger-nanny considering that they had already offered her the choice of three situations, none of which suited her, and it had been made perfectly plain that she was no longer wanted in the Pets' Corner.

She tried to leave the cage but every door in the Big Cats' House was fast locked, so she moped anxiously in a corner until the director of the gardens and the head keeper arrived to look at her.

'Well, you have led us a dance!' the head keeper said, letting her out and taking off her hat. 'We thought you had got lost!'

'I'm very sorry, sir. I was only fixing myself up with a situation,' said Tiger-nanny. 'I am now nurse to Miss Mandoline Harper's three children. If you will let me go back to them now, sir, it is time to get them up from their rests.'

'Steady now, steady!' said the director of the gardens. 'I don't think you realize, my dear, that you are a very valuable young tiger-cub!'

'Yes, sir. Forty mothers at the employment bureau were anxious to get my services!' Tiger-nanny agreed modestly. The director laughed.

'And you may be surprised to hear that this morning we had an offer to buy you from Bellamy's Circus!' he said. 'And another one from Lord Clanhaddock the Elder who is opening a Safari Park in the Isle of Flugg. And everyone knows you are the most popular animal in the gardens. We really can't spare you to go and be a children's nurse.'

Tiger-nanny bowed her head, but her backbone stiffened, and ever so slightly her tail lashed to and fro.

'That is the career I would prefer, sir,' she replied politely. The director's stare and the keeper's fell before the purposeful gaze of her large, limpid eyes.

The keeper spoke first.

'You had better talk some sense into her!' he told her mother, pushing Tiger-nanny back into the cage. They left the Big Cats' House in earnest conversation while Tiger-nanny marched up and down, up and down, paying no attention to her mother's admonitions. Her heart beat in anguish at the thought of her three charges, who trusted her, waking from their rest to find her absent. She was afraid they might massacre poor Miss Bankes. She was glad she had given little Salvatore his blanket to love.

The long afternoon dragged by and Tiger-nanny fretted in the Big Cats' House. She had not lived there since she was a tiny cub. During the whole of her childhood she had had the freedom of the gardens. Now she wondered how her mother could possibly seem peaceful and satisfied in such close confinement.

Crowds poured in to look at her. Fanned by the BBC broadcast her popularity had doubled in an hour.

'She's back again!' was on every tongue in tones of vast relief. People went clamouring to the head keeper to ask if she could be returned to the Pets' Corner.

'We'll see. The director will have to make up his mind about it,' was all the keeper could tell them.

Tiger-nanny took no notice of the public or their noisy welcome. Up and down, up and down she paced, thinking of the children. She wondered if she could make a dash for it at feeding time and slip out under the keeper's arm. But he was ready for her and fended her off.

'Poor thing! She doesn't want to eat! Perhaps she's sick!' said the public, watching the Big Cats tear their meat apart while Tiger-nanny moped in a corner.

Just before closing time, when the Big Cats' House was nearly empty, a commotion was heard at the entrance and three children burst into the passage in front of the cages.

Tiger-nanny leapt up from her corner, for the children were, of course, Samantha, Julius and Salvatore, the youngest trailing his pet blanket which was grubby once more with his tears and the dust and grime of the journey to the Zoological Gardens.

'She's *there*!' shouted Julius.

'Oh, Tiger-nanny, darling, we thought we'd die!' shrieked Samantha.

'We waited and waited. Miss Bankes is in *hysterics*! Salvatore *bit* her! We knew you must be at the zoo, so after tea we got a taxi, but you weren't at the Pets' Corner and they wouldn't tell us anything! How do you open that door at the back? You've got to come home with us this minute!'

'Sorry, miss, but it's quite impossible!' said the head keeper, suddenly appearing at Samantha's elbow. 'Director's orders.'

'Silly fool!' said Julius very rudely in French. 'Do you know who we are?' he continued in a haughty English voice. 'We are Mandoline Harper's children and this is our nanny.'

'Sorry, son, but there's been no contract made for her so far as I've heard of it,' said the keeper calmly. 'This tiger is the property of the Zoological Gardens.' Salvatore began to bawl.

'Stupid! Stupid!' screamed Samantha to everyone in general. 'Come to the director's office!' she said to her brothers and fled from the Big Cats' House, dragging the sobbing Salvatore by the hand.

The head keeper shrugged his shoulders and closed the outer door of the Big Cats' House with a key. It was closing time for the public anyway.

The director, of course, was not in his office. He had gone home some time before. The children had to go home too. For a while they battered and screamed in vain at the closed door of the Big Cats' House, but a bevy of keepers bore down on them and slowly, inexorably shepherded them to the gate. 'You can come back in the morning,' they told them. 'The director may be here by then.'

Mandoline Harper had barely returned, exhausted, from the set, when her children burst in upon her, hysterical with grief.

'They shut us out! They shut her in! She's ours! She isn't theirs! We've paid for her! We went to the director but he was out! We went to the employment bureau but it was shut! We went to the police but they sent us home! The taxi is waiting! We've had it for two and a half hours! Can somebody pay for it?'

'Darlings! Darlings!' said their exhausted mother under the weight of Salvatore sprawled across her chest. 'I'm dead, my darlings, I really am! Go and tell Elwyn all about it!'

They began all over again. Lucien came in in the middle. When he heard the gist of it he very sensibly told them that nothing could be done that night. 'We'll put it straight in the morning,' he promised little Torie, who was choking with grief and ingested tufts of his blanket.

The children believed Lucien, who made promises as seldom as possible, but kept them when he did.

They dined in a subdued manner with their parents and went to bed around midnight, without washing.

In the morning they sat at the end of Mandoline's bed while first Elwyn Bankes and finally Lucien spoke to the director of the Zoological Gardens on the telephone.

'It seems,' Lucien relayed at last to the waiting children, 'that they have already had big offers for the tiger from Bellamy's Circus and the Safari Park at Flugg.'

'Is that all?' said Mandoline, opening her eyes with relief. 'Well, get Billy on to it and make them a bigger offer still. And get off my bed, kids, you're killing me.'

The children trailed round mournfully in dressing-gowns while Mandoline's press agent negotiated with the Zoological Gardens and they waited for the result to come through. If their hearts were full of hope this was soon dashed. Around midday Billy Pullen, Mandoline's agent, appeared, looking rueful. It seemed that an agreement had already been drawn up and signed since breakfast-time with Lord Clanhaddock the Elder who wanted Tiger-nanny for his Safari Park.

The children burst into tears and were inconsolable. Lucien hurried to the set and Mandoline, dressing hastily, followed him. Samantha, Julius and Salvatore were left to Miss Bankes. To her great relief they took a taxi to the zoo, but were soon back again because the Big Cats' House was closed for the afternoon.

Mooching about the streets Julius bought an evening paper, and there on the front page saw a picture of the three of them, tear-stained and tattered, leaving the gates of the Zoological Gardens on the evening before. They were so accustomed to being photographed and to the Press following them on all occasions that the picture hardly surprised them, but the headlines did:

'FILM STAR'S CHILDREN DEPRIVED OF THEIR PET!' they ran, and then 'MANDY HARPER'S adored adopted tiger, friend and guardian of her young sons and daughter, has been sold away to the isolation of Lord Clanhaddock's new Safari Park on the Island of Flugg. "My children are broken

hearted," Miss Harper told the Press today. "The youngest, Salvatore, has been ill ever since their pet was taken from them. I do not think anything will ever take her place in his heart." '

'There!' said Julius in triumph. 'Good old Mandy! Good old Sally! Let's see if that doesn't fetch Lord Clanhaddock!'

It did. The next morning the papers announced that a cable had been received from Lord Clanhaddock the Elder renouncing his claim to the tiger in favour of the grieving children. The Press stormed the apartment but the children were all asleep, worn out by their day of woe. Mandoline received the Press looking motherly and beautiful in bed. She had offered the gardens a much larger sum than Lord Clanhaddock's for the tiger, she said, so everybody was going to be happy ever after. She promised the 'dear boys of the Press' that Tiger-nanny should give them an interview when she came home. And they could take some pictures of her setting out with the family on their afternoon walk.

But before the children had had their breakfast and finished rejoicing another blow arrived from the Zoological Gardens. The director himself rang up Lucien, who had not gone to work, since everything was in a state of chaos and Mandoline wanted to be available for the Press. The director explained with much embarrassment that the young tiger cub refused to come back.

'Refuses to come back? What do you mean?' said the film director, astounded. 'She seemed perfectly happy here.'

'It's the terms,' the director explained awkwardly.

'The terms? What *are* the terms? I don't mind what I pay to keep the kids happy. Double the terms!' said Lucien impatiently.

'It isn't that,' said the director unhappily. 'She says – she says she won't sell her independence at any price. She says she is a children's nurse, registered at the employment bureau, and she will come for fair wages, but nobody is going to buy or sell her.'

'Oh, good grief!' said Lucien in exasperation. 'I'll pay her as much or as little as she asks for, it doesn't matter to me.''

'No, sir,' the director agreed. 'But you will remember, sir, that Lord Clanhaddock offered us three thousand pounds.'

The film director did see.

'Well, I'll leave it to my agent to fix it up with you,' he said. 'I'm sure we can come to some understanding over this.'

'Yes, yes,' agreed the director of the Zoological Gardens, 'but the tiger insists on a proper contract, guaranteeing her freedom to leave the post if she is not satisfied with the position.'

'Well, let her have the contract then!' snapped the film director. 'I'll pay four thousand pounds to you privately and I'll sign any contract she likes that will bring her back to the children, otherwise we'll never have any peace and quiet again. As a matter of fact they get tired of anything in a week, so I guess nobody is going to break their hearts either way.'

The contract was duly signed and Tiger-nanny came back from the zoo in a taxi. She put all the children into a bath, washed out Fluff, and saw to it that they were all in bed by seven o'clock.

'Now tell us stories about the little children you used to look after in your previous posts,' said Samantha.

'The awful ones, not the good ones,' added Julius.

'I had no previous post. It would be lies to say I had,' said Tiger-nanny.

'Then tell us lots of lies,' said Julius.

'Never,' said Tiger-nanny. 'I may not be very experienced but I know it is wrong to tell lies to children. But I will tell you about some very, very naughty little children that used to visit the gardens.'

'And did the tigers eat them up?' said Julius hopefully.

'Of course not, Julius. I am afraid you have a very vulgar mind,' said Tiger-nanny, tucking him in. 'They were very naughty little children indeed, and their names were Julius, Samantha and Salvatore . . .'

4 · *A baby for Tiger-nanny*

Tiger-nanny was not simply being proud when she refused to sell away her independence, or have the gardens sell it away for her. In fact, if Lord Clanhaddock had bought her, or Bellamy's Circus, she would have submitted meekly to being sent away from home, and the question of payment would not have come into it, though it might have broken her heart to have to give up her life's ambition.

But she knew she must keep some hold over Mandoline Harper's children, and the threat of leaving them was by far the best one. If they realized that she was not going to stand unlimited bad conduct then they would be much more likely to behave well, and she was determined to stay with them until little Salvatore was old enough to go to school and the others had been trained into rather better ways. But deep down in her heart was the longing to push out a pram, as a children's nurse has every right to do. Little Salvatore had kicked his pram to pieces long ago.

The children settled down into a peaceful routine, and after a brief press conference the family was left alone to get on with its private life. A protest march of mothers headed by the forty mums who had protested so vehemently against Mandoline's right to employ Tiger-nanny, bearing the slogans 'Give Mandy's Children back their Pet!' and 'Rights for Film Star's Babies!' fell rather flat when they arrived at the zoo gates and heard that Tiger-nanny was back again at her job. A stone was thrown at Lord Clanhaddock's London house but fortunately missed the windows.

The Big Cats' House was re-opened and Tiger-nanny's mother became famous overnight.

'Tiger-nanny was born here!' was painted on a new board hung underneath the cage.

Fresh excitement blazed up when Tiger-nanny took the children walking in the park, Salvatore on his tricycle, the elder two walking one on either side of her with their hands wound about Tiger-nanny's neck. Fortunately all of them were used to being stared at and took no notice at all.

When the children went to swing on the swings or play beside the lake Tiger-nanny was surprised to find that other children's nannies made advances to her. She had expected them to ignore her or even resent her presence among their ranks, but instead they invited her to come and sit on their benches, while keeping their babies rather apart, with the pram hoods up. Tiger-nanny admired the babies from a distance and asked questions about their care that flattered the nurses, who had approached her because they hoped she would gossip about the film star, Mandoline Harper, but Tiger-nanny was most professionally quiet upon that subject.

'Yes, madam is working very hard on her film' and 'Yes, madam is very devoted to her children,' was all they could get out of her. She was a nice little thing, they told each other, and she didn't give herself airs just because she was employed by a film star.

The children improved daily in every possible way. Their clothes were mended, their hairs were washed, their underclothes were changed and their teeth were brushed. Tiger-nanny took them all three to the dentist, and sat over them while he worked with his drill.

'I congratulate you, Nanny!' said the dentist, when he was finished. 'I thought all film stars' children were little horrors. These are very well brought up indeed.'

'Yes,' said Tiger-nanny, putting the tooth that the dentist had extracted into a little polythene envelope for Salvatore to keep. She led the children away.

On her half days she went back to the zoo to see her family. She was always welcome in the Pets' Corner now, and once it was known which days she was free there was sure to be a record attendance.

Her mother was affectionate but not very interested. She was expecting more babies and hoped Tiger-nanny would come back and help to look after them.

'What will you do when the film is finished and the family moves elsewhere?' she asked.

'I expect I shall go too,' said Tiger-nanny. 'Little Salvatore has nearly stopped sucking his fingers and I hope by the time he goes to school he will go to sleep without his blanket.'

Mandoline Harper and her husband were wholly satisfied and delighted with Tiger-nanny. The children had never been so orderly or well behaved. Mandoline acquired even more publicity now she had a tiger for a nurse, and her press agent saw to it that the children did not steal it all away.

'Keep it up, old girl, keep it up!' Lucien said, patting Tiger-nanny round the head. 'We'll raise your wages whenever you ask for it! It's just up to you, old girl, none other!'

Tiger-nanny asked for a modest rise. She was paying back the employment bureau for her share of the contract and she gave the balance to the Royal Society for the Prevention of Cruelty to Animals. She had been so fortunate, she thought, in getting such a happy position, while many animals were miserable and did not even get enough to eat.

She tolerated her employers and Miss Bankes who was still half frightened of her but much more frightened of being left without her, and she loved the children dearly, whether they were naughty or whether they were good. It gave her real pleasure to hear Julius getting on better with his stepfather. Sometimes he even called him Daddo.

'Do you like us, Tiger-nanny?' Samantha asked, snuggling up to her.

'I like you when you are good,' said Tiger-nanny.

'But don't you love us when we are naughty?' asked Samantha.

'I always love you whether you are naughty or good,' said Tiger-nanny. 'But I don't *like* you when you are naughty.'

'Like God,' said Samantha comfortably.

'Perhaps,' said Tiger-nanny.

'Julius sucks bull's-eyes while he is saying his prayers,' Samantha said. 'God can't possibly like him to do that.'

'Tell tale tit
Your tongue shall be slit
And all the tigers in the town
Shall have a little bit!'

sang Tiger-nanny.

'Oh, Tiger-nanny, how rude!' said Samantha, shocked. 'It never said that.'

'I know it didn't,' said Tiger-nanny happily. 'But I thought it sounded funnier that way.'

They all giggled and Julius handed round the bull's-eyes.

'Are you happy with us, Tiger-nanny?' Samantha was asking nearly every day.

'Yes, dear, I am very happy.'

'Absolutely, terrifically, totally happy?' Samantha demanded.

'I think I have never been so happy before,' Tiger-nanny said truthfully, ironing little shirts.

'And will you stay with us for ever and ever and ever?'

'Well,' Tiger-nanny hesitated. 'Perhaps not for ever and ever and ever.'

'Why not, Tiger-nanny?'

'You will get too old for me,' said Tiger-nanny, straightening collars.

'Oh no, *never*! Mummy's nurse stayed till she was dead. Nurse Jones, I mean, not Mummy. And she'd had Mummy since she was born.'

'Ah!' said Tiger-nanny wistfully.

'Why do you say *Ah*! like that?' the children cried. 'Do you wish you had had us since we were born?'

'Yes, my dears,' said Tiger-nanny quietly.

'Why, what's wrong with us now?'

'Well, to tell you the truth,' said Tiger-nanny very gently, 'I would – some day – like to have the opportunity to push a pram.'

Early in the morning Samantha rushed into her mother's room and bounced upon the bed.

'Darling – you are killing me!' Mandoline wailed. 'Go back and ask Nanny to give you your breakfast. It's only just past midnight, I swear it is.'

'Mummy, you've got to listen to me!' Samantha shouted, so loudly that Lucien came in from his dressing-room. 'Tiger-nanny is going to leave!'

'Oh *no*!' said Mandoline Harper with such heartfelt despair in her voice that her husband's heart too dropped into his boots.

'For crying out loud!' he exclaimed. 'Last week I raised her wages and she's only just come!'

'It's not wages!' Samantha exclaimed with scorn. 'She thinks all this talk about money is quite disgustingly vulgar. She doesn't want wages. She wants a baby to look after.'

'A baby!' said Mandoline blankly. 'But she's got Salvatore!'

'Mummy!' said Samantha, forcing herself to be patient. 'Torie is *four years old*! He doesn't have a bottle, he doesn't wear nappies and he doesn't ride in a pram. Nannies love all these things. They have a right to them.'

'Well, babies don't grow on trees, old girl!' Lucien broke in unwisely as Mandoline sank back on her pillows murmuring: 'If nanny leaves and I have to take on the children again I shall just die, I know I shall.'

'Of course babies don't grow on trees!' Samantha snapped, rounding angrily on her stepfather. 'But you and Mummy had Salvatore, why can't you just have another one for Tiger-nanny?'

'Oh, darling, I should die if I had another baby, I know I should,' moaned Mandoline Harper. 'And there's the new picture we're going to make. When this one's done I have to go over to Matsumundu and make one there.'

Lucien gave a snort. 'We haven't got permission to go into the country yet, much less make a picture there,' he grunted, 'and I'm not taking the kids out of England without a nurse. They can all three go to boarding-school.'

Samantha at once went into hysterics in which her mother joined. Tiger-nanny came bounding in with only just enough time to knock at the bedroom door.

'Samantha! Madam! What is the matter, madam?' she asked in some anxiety.

'Samantha has been telling her mother she ought to have another baby,' Lucien explained curtly. 'I don't know what you have been teaching them in the nursery.'

Tiger-nanny looked very offended.

'I am sorry, sir, I don't understand,' she said. 'Come into the bathroom, Samantha and put your head under the tap. It strikes me that you have been poking your nose into other people's business.' As Samantha preceded her, sobbing wildly, Tiger-nanny turned back and faced Lucien.

'If I do not give satisfaction, sir, I can always go back to the gardens,' she said acidly, before closing the door very gently behind her.

'There, you see, you have upset her and now she'll leave!' wailed Mandoline Harper. 'And it takes months and months and months to have a baby! We shall have all the children round our necks and I'll never be able to make the Matsumundu film, and if I do have a baby I'll have to bring it up all by myself!'

The next moment Tiger-nanny was standing at her elbow holding a cup of hot tea.

'Drink this, madam,' she said kindly. 'It will make you feel much better. I have sent Samantha back to bed.'

5 · *Plans for the future*

But from that moment things began to go, not wrong, but not quite so well. Samantha flounced about refusing to apologize to her mother, so Tiger-nanny was cold and distant with her. Julius baited Miss Bankes and teased Salvatore. He went back to calling Lucien Stepdad on every occasion. Salvatore whined. Mandoline Harper quarrelled with everybody on the set including her husband, came home and went to bed for a week.

The fault was not really Samantha's and Tiger-nanny knew it. The family was under a certain strain.

It was Lucien's dearest wish to direct a film in Matsumundu, that most reactionary of Eastern states whose ruler so strongly disapproved of Western habits that he would not even have a cinema in the country. The story had been written, with the leading part in it especially created for Mandoline Harper.

The country itself was unique. Its natural beauty, architecture and the splendour of its people would be very difficult to reproduce in a film studio, or in any other country in the world. The film would have a double success with Mandoline in the lead if it could be proved to have been actually filmed in Matsumundu.

But so far permission was not obtainable, though Lucien had tried in all directions to find a way in.

Very recently there had been a revolution in Matsumundu which had quickly been suppressed but a rumour had spread that the people had revolted because they wanted to have cinemas and film-shows like any other country, and while the army was restoring order the ruler, King Timpa, had sent his wife and three-month-old crown prince to England to keep the baby heir to the throne safe until things were quiet again. He sent for his wife to come back again, but it seemed prudent to leave the baby out of the country for a little longer because there was always the fear that he might be seized and held hostage against the people's demands for a cinema.

The care and kindness that his wife and child had received in England had made the king feel much more kindly towards that country, and Lucien hoped that once the baby was safely home again, negotiations for making the film in Matsumundu might be reopened. He sent first-night invitations to the queen for all the newest films in London and noticed that she enjoyed them very much.

She returned home full of enthusiasm for the cinema, but forgot them all in waiting and pining for her baby son.

All this happened while Mandoline was sulking in her bed, refusing to go back on the set and telling her husband repeatedly that she would just lie down and die if he tried to make her.

She really was very exhausted after the making of the long film and Tiger-nanny kept the children away from her as much as possible, offering Mandoline fruit salts and hot-water bottles and telling her to just lie down and sleep it off.

Miss Bankes kept visitors from the door, and for once Mandoline was very glad to have a rest. When a notice appeared in the papers: 'MANDY HARPER IS RESTING FROM THE SET', she began to feel she deserved the break and took another week in bed.

On the thirteenth day her press agent arrived at an unexpected hour and shut himself up for a long talk with Lucien and Miss Bankes. Julius tried to listen at the door in vain.

'All I heard was something Lucien muttered about "I can't cope with the little devil",' he announced. 'I suppose he was talking about *me*.'

'Julius, I am ashamed of you!' Tiger-nanny exclaimed, lashing her tail in a way they had come to recognize as her angry manner. 'Listeners never hear good of themselves. There was a little boy who listened at a keyhole and a wasp came out and stung him in the ear.'

'Was the wasp listening too?' asked Salvatore.

When the children were in bed and Tiger-nanny

was letting down a dress of Samantha's, Lucien appeared at the nursery door and politely asked her to step into Mandoline Harper's bedroom.

Mandoline was sitting up in bed looking dramatic, as if she were learning a new part. Miss Bankes, beside her, seemed anxious. Billy Pullen, her press agent, and Lucien both looked very serious.

'Tiger-nanny,' Lucien began. 'We have a proposition before us that may affect all our careers.'

Tiger-nanny waited patiently.

'You may have heard,' Lucien continued, 'of a country called Matsumundu where I am anxious to make a film?' Tiger-nanny had heard of little else for several days.

'And perhaps you know,' Lucien continued, 'that the baby prince of that country is at present in England.'

'Parted from his mother,' Tiger-nanny agreed, with the slight purr in her throat that came into it when she thought about babies.

'And it is very, very important that he shall soon be returned to her,' Lucien went on. 'At first it was safer for him to be here, but now his own country is quiet again, while there have been hints that certain people outside Matsumundu would be glad to get possession of him and hold him to ransom against their demands.'

'It sounds rather dangerous for a little baby,' said Tiger-nanny anxiously.

'The ambassador from Matsumundu has been in touch with me,' said Lucien. 'He thinks that if we could get the baby safely home to his parents there would be no difficulty in getting permission from King Timpa to make a film in the country, as I am so anxious to do.'

'That would be very nice,' said Tiger-nanny.

'The difficulty is, how to do it,' said Billy Pullen. Miss Bankes looked more anxious than ever.

'I just can't bear the thought of that poor baby being kidnapped!' said Mandoline. 'It just kills me!'

'The baby is quite safe at present in a private house in the country,' Lucien said. 'But we have a strong suspicion that some spies from Matsumundu have found out where the house is. The baby must be removed to a safer place as soon as possible. The question is, where can it be hidden?'

'Here!' said Tiger-nanny, her large, green, gentle eyes shining with delight.

'There you are!' said Mandoline, half fretful, half pleased, 'Samantha said you wanted a baby and now you've got one! You'll stay with us now, won't you, Tiger-nanny?'

'Lucien, our Mandy has taken the trick,' Billy Pullen said excitedly. 'We can get the baby out of the country house all right, but how else could we make it disappear? Why, just like that of course!' and he snapped his fingers. 'One baby vanishes and another one appears. Mandoline Harper has a baby! Gee,

Miss Bankes, do you think you can go out and buy a pram?'

'But what happens then?' asked Mandoline. 'Do we keep the baby?'

'No,' said Billy Pullen. 'What you've got to do next is to get permission to start making a movie in Matsumundu. I'll see to it that their ambassador knows just the reason why. Then the baby and its nannie and the kids go on ahead while you finish making our present picture over here – that'll kind of avert suspicion, they might begin to wonder if the whole party takes off at once – and in next to no time you'll be on the new set over there.'

'Sounds good to me,' said Lucien. Mandoline was delighted.

'Nanny will take care of them all. I simply hate travelling on aeroplanes with children. It kills me,' she said.

'Excuse me,' said Tiger-nanny. 'But I have never travelled on an aeroplane in my life.'

'You'll love it,' said Mandoline Harper.

'I had not thought about leaving the country,' said Tiger-nanny. 'Only the Zoological Gardens. And I am not sure how the climate will suit the children.'

'The kids have travelled all over, all their lives,' said Mandoline. 'Salvatore was born in an aeroplane, going to Helsinki. You don't mean to tell me you don't want to go? Oh, Tiger-nanny! Don't treat me like that, you'll kill me!'

'I would like to discuss it in the gardens first, please, madam,' said Tiger-nanny.

'Now look here, old girl,' said Lucien, putting a large brown hand under Tiger-nanny's chin and rubbing it. 'The gardens have nothing to do with it. Your contract says you are free to do as you like. Free, see?'

'Yes,' said Tiger-nanny, removing her chin. 'I was thinking about my family and their feelings.'

'Well, you will have to be quick about it,' said the director. 'There really isn't any time to spare. I shall have to tell the ambassador and we ought to get the baby into safe-keeping as quickly as possible. Call a taxi, Miss Bankes, to take Tiger-nanny to the zoo. I can rely on you of course, Tiger-nanny, to say nothing except that you have been asked to take the children abroad.'

The mention of the baby made up Tiger-nanny's mind before she left the apartment, but she wanted to tell her mother and the head keeper what plans were in store for her immediate future, so she jumped into the taxi and was admitted to the Zoological Gardens by a side gate.

The head keeper welcomed her. 'You couldn't have come at a better moment, Tigs!' he told her, leading the way to the Big Cats' House. 'Your mother had five cubs this morning.'

Tiger-nanny flew into the cage where her mother lay on clean straw, shining with pride. Beside her rolled five fat, fluffy lumps of fur with soft helpless paws and innocent faces. Their small mouths opened and whimpered, they searched for food, sucked noisily and slept again. Tiger-nanny's heart swelled in one great surge of love for them; she bent down and licked them lovingly one by one.

'Five of them! Five babies!' she breathed, purring with rapture.

'It's all very well for you to purr over them!' said her mother with tears in her eyes. 'I'll never be able to rear that lot. I simply haven't got enough milk and some of the poor little darlings are sure to die, unless they are reared by hand.'

'By hand?' purred Tiger-nanny.

'Bottles,' said her mother. 'It's hard on them but I don't want them to die: I thought perhaps you might like to do it.'

'Oh yes! Yes!' purred Tiger-nanny, embracing

as many of the little cubs as she could envelop with her paws and tongue. 'Oh, I would! I would!'

'I thought you were in a bit of a hurry to leave home!' her mother said accusingly. 'With all this baby-care business you have been studying you ought to be able to cope with two or three of your little brothers and sisters. I'll nurse the weakest – that little stripy fellow and his sister who is so like him, but you can do the best you can for the others.'

Suddenly Tiger-nanny jerked up her head and stopped short in the middle of her kissings and lickings. In her mind's eye she saw the three children sleeping in their beds in Mandoline Harper's apartment – handsome Julius sprawled across his pillows with his naughty face all smoothed out soft and guileless as if he were still only three years old. And warm-hearted, loving Samantha lying on her back, a half smile on her lips as she dreamed of foreign lands – or was it the gossip she lapped up from the set? And Salvatore, as fat and golden and vulnerable as these same baby cubs – who had hardly untwined his arms from round her neck to say goodnight before he was asleep, muttering 'See you in the mornin', Tiger-nan!' because nothing on earth would have persuaded him that Tiger-nanny would ever let him down. And in the further distance came the more elusive picture of a small helpless baby, parted from his mother, threatened by its father's enemies, needing above all the protection of a tiger-nanny to care for it and take it home.

While she was in this terrible state of perplexity the head keeper came back to the cage.

'Splendid sight, aren't they, your little brothers and sisters?' he said cheerfully, rubbing the cubs behind the ears. 'How are you feeling, Duchess? Rather a handful for you to cope with, I think. In fact I don't think you will be able to do it all by yourself. But don't worry, old girl. Your babies will be all right. My old labrador will take two or three of them, she's lost her puppies and she'll love to raise them. My kids will have some fun out of them too.'

Tiger-nanny's heart leapt with relief and thankfulness. She kissed all the little tigers over again and prepared to leave.

'I only wanted to tell you that my family wish me to travel abroad,' she told her mother.

'Really? How you do get around!' said her mother, briskly applying herself to her cubs. 'I hope you will have a nice time.'

'Better than Bellamy's Circus – eh?' said the keeper, digging Tiger-nanny in the ribs. She cantered back to the taxi.

6 · *The baby*

There remained to tell the children. Tiger-nanny felt perfectly convinced that the elder two could be trusted.

'It will be good for them to feel they are old enough to keep a secret,' she told their parents.

'Well, if you think so, Tiger-nanny, I am ready to agree,' said the film director.

'The strain will kill me!' wailed Mandoline. 'And what with all my friends thinking I've had a baby . . .'

'I think, madam, it might be best for Salvatore to think so too,' said Tiger-nanny. 'I don't approve of telling lies to little children, but perhaps just for the few days the baby is in the house, it might be wiser to let him think what he likes about it. When we get to Matsumundu I can explain. One can hardly expect such a very little boy to keep it to himself.'

'He's the only one with any brains among the lot of them,' said Salvatore's father, causing Mandoline to fizz with indignation.

So it was that two days later a car arrived at the apartment very late at night, and in the morning the rooms resounded to the sound of a baby's wailing.

'What's that?' said Salvatore, brushing his teeth.

'It's the baby,' said Julius.

'What baby?' said Salvatore.

'*The* baby, you drip.'

'There,' said Salvatore, rather crossly. 'I knew Mummy was going to have a baby because Tiger-nanny wanted one. Is it a boy or a girl?'

The baby was a little golden-brown baby with dark eyes.

Tiger-nanny and Samantha almost fought each other to look after it.

Julius was indifferent and Salvatore openly hostile. He did not like Tiger-nanny to be giving the baby so much attention.

'Why can't Mummy look after it?' he grumbled.

Mandoline Harper, tired of being in bed, was facing another week of idleness to keep up appearances.

'Don't bring it near me!' she begged Tiger-nanny. 'I can't stand them when they are as small as that.'

'I can't either,' said Salvatore.

The morning papers arrived together with masses and masses of flowers for Mandoline.

'MANDY'S SECRET!' the headlines said, and 'THE BABY THAT STOLE THE SHOW!'

'Mandoline Harper has been off the set for the past two weeks,' Billy Pullen had carefully instructed the Press to announce. 'Late last night the cause was apparent. A baby has arrived at Mandoline's home. Now Mandoline's Tiger-nanny will have a pram to push in the park at last!'

The pram chosen by Miss Bankes had indeed arrived, white and silver. Samantha crooned over it and Tiger-nanny said it was very nice indeed. She could hardly wait to wheel the baby out in the park. But the three-month-old baby heir to the state of Matsumundu did not really look like a film star's new-born child, and he had a voice like a fog-horn.

Tiger-nanny did take him out, but she had her own back on the park nurses who had kept their babies out of her reach, by putting muslin all over the hood and refusing to let anyone look inside. Julius guarded them. He was very proud of the secret that had been entrusted to him and took the situation very seriously indeed.

Samantha was almost too besotted with baby worship to be any help at all, except with bottle feeding.

And when the other nannies asked Salvatore if he liked his little brother, Mandoline's youngest turned away his head and said loudly: 'He's not my brother at all!''

'Isn't he jealous, bless him!' the nurses said to Tiger-nanny. 'They're always like that at his age.'

At the end of a fortnight there was nothing more about Mandoline's new baby in the papers and she was tired of staying in bed.

‘I’m going back on the set if it kills me,’ she announced.

Meanwhile very favourable and secret negotiations had been going on between the state of Matsumundu and the film company in London. It had been decided that the day Mandoline went back on the set the children with Tiger-nanny should fly out to Matsumundu. The Press would be likely to be more interested in Mandoline Harper than in themselves, and Lucien hoped he might get them on to the plane before they were observed. The tickets were bought, and the little heir and his belongings were packed into a travelling cot protected by a muslin veil.

Mandoline bade them a hysterical farewell in the morning.

'Partings kill me,' she sobbed, 'I'll see you in two weeks' time, my beautifuls, don't forget Mummy, do what Nanny tells you, kiss me again, all of you; I think the Press is here, give me a hug, Torie baby; oh no, it's the taxi man . . .'

'You kissed my Fluff. Why don't you kiss baby brother?' said Salvatore curiously.

'I did, I did, precious. I gave him fifty kisses!' exclaimed Mandoline, avoiding the travelling basket as she embraced Salvatore yet again.

'No, you didn't. He hasn't got any lipstick on him.' said Salvatore, lifting the muslin. 'You can have Fluff till we get into the aeroplane,' he told the baby, pushing the blanket into his clutching hands. 'Tiger-nanny, I've given my Fluff to the baby.'

'You are a very kind little boy,' said Tiger-nanny, which was just what Salvatore wished her to say.

Lucien and the press agent drove them to the airport. All was new and exciting to Tiger-nanny. She was disappointed that the children showed so little enthusiasm.

'Look at the aeroplanes!' she cried as they arrived.

'We've seen thousands of aeroplanes,' said Julius crossly. 'I do wish we could have gone by bus.'

Tiger-nanny and the children waited in the car while Lucien and the press agent went to weigh and clear the luggage. They came back perfectly grey with distress.

'What's the matter, Daddo?' asked Julius. 'What's happened to him, Bill?'

'It's Tiger-nanny,' said his stepfather, speaking very fast and avoiding Tiger-nanny's gaze. 'It seems it is absolutely impossible for her to travel by air unless she's in a crate.'

'Oh, look here!' expostulated Julius.

'Oh, *no*!' said Samantha in horror.

'If it will make things easier I am quite ready to travel in a crate,' said Tiger-nanny meekly, 'only I don't think Samantha could look after the others *and* the baby without me.'

'No, I couldn't,' Samantha agreed.

'Impossible. Impossible. It is absolutely essential that you should travel with the children,' said Lucien with determination. 'We'll go home and think it out. I don't think anyone has noticed us and I'm sure we will be able to work out a way to get round the problem.'

They returned to the apartment. Mandoline's shrieks of dismay when she returned from the set to find them there might have led anyone to think she was sorry to see them back again, but she assured them it was only the shock that was killing her, and the spectacle of Tiger-nanny dressing up in the long grey coat and little felt hat with which she had so nearly deceived the clerk at the employment bureau.

'I think it will do,' Lucien said to Billy Pullen. 'And if she keeps on her woolly gloves and wears black shoes, nobody will ever take her for a tiger.'

The baby prince screamed and roared when he saw Tiger-nanny dressed up, and refused to take his evening bottle, but presently he accepted her, eyeing her suspiciously from the arms of Samantha, who had joyfully fed him in Tiger-nanny's place.

'I think he's quite right to scream. You look awful in those clothes,' said Julius. 'You look almost human. And I don't know any human being in the world who looks as beautiful as you do when you are not dressed up, Tiger-nanny.'

Tiger-nanny blushed inside at this compliment from Julius.

'Well, this isn't a time to worry about our looks, dear,' was all she said.

7 · *Hi-jacked*

It was decided that Tiger-nanny and the children should go to the airport by taxi the next morning in case Lucien's big car had been recognized.

'I believe somebody has been watching the house all night,' Julius announced, eating breakfast in his mother's room.

'Oh, no, Julius, don't! I can't bear it!' shrieked Mandoline, collapsing on her pillows. 'What did you see?'

'It was a policeman,' said Julius slyly with his mouth full. 'But quite early this morning somebody came up to the door and then went away again.'

'Julius, you're killing me!' Mandoline gasped.

'It was the milkman,' Julius proceeded wickedly. 'But shortly after that somebody came up the steps and opened the letter-box flap just long enough to peep inside and – '

'*It was the postman!*' Samantha and he shouted together, while their mother cried and laughed and expostulated and Tiger-nanny came into the bedroom dressed to travel.

'What is Tiger-nanny wearing Miss Bankes's clothes for?' asked Salvatore, who had been in bed when Tiger-nanny had tried on her clothes.

'It's so they won't put her in a crate on the aeroplane,' Julius explained to him. 'She's travelling in the disguise of a lady, not a tiger.'

'Well, why can't she dress in pretty clothes and smell nice like Mummy?' Salvatore wanted to know. Nobody seemed to know the answer.

'Because I want to look and smell like a Tiger-nanny,' said Tiger-nanny.

'I thought you did,' Salvatore agreed happily.

They were in the taxi at last, speeding to the airport, and very discreetly positioned along the route was an escort of police.

'I did see somebody watching the house early this morning!' Julius whispered to Samantha. 'And when he saw me looking through the curtains he walked away.'

'Well, nobody can really hurt the baby now,' Samantha said. 'Not with all those policemen and Tiger-nanny around.'

This time they boarded the aeroplane without a hitch.

Julius dealt with the luggage, using the competence of an experienced traveller. The passport officer bustled them through the barrier, hardly looking at their passports.

The baby prince lay sleeping like a dusky rose, his

travelling cot swinging between Samantha and Tiger-nanny's grey-gloved woolly paw. The air hostess welcomed them all aboard the plane to Matsumundu. 'Hullo, Julius!' she said. 'I saw you and your sister and brother on the Far East flight. And who is this, I'd like to know?'

Tiger-nanny's fur began to twitch with apprehension, but Julius carried off the situation with great coolness.

'It's the baby,' he replied calmly.

'Well!' said the air hostess. 'Has Mandy Harper had a baby? I missed that one. Have you got a little brother or a little sister, dear?' she bent over Salvatore, peeping into the travelling-cot.

'No, I haven't,' said Salvatore.

The other passengers were streaming up the gangway now. To Tiger-nanny's relief the hostess had to go and look after them.

'Go into the rear compartment with the children, Nanny!' she called back. 'I'll come and see you presently!'

Several passengers had heard her loud reference to Mandoline Harper and were looking backwards into the compartment that Tiger-nanny and the children had been given to themselves. Tiger-nanny heard questions being asked as they settled themselves in, and wished that she had asked the air hostess to keep the information to herself. But it was too late, and really there was nothing to fear now that they were all safely together on board the plane.

Just so long as nobody recognized her under her grey coat, grey gloves and tidy little round felt hat. As the crew came aboard, Tiger-nanny turned her back and busied herself unpacking the case containing the little prince's bottles.

'He's got my Fluff!' said Salvatore, pulling it away from under the sleeping baby.

'You gave it to him!' said Samantha accusingly.

'Only till we got into the plane,' said Salvatore self-righteously as the baby began to cry. It cried with the healthy volume of a three-and-a-half-months-old future ruler, and babies in Matsumundu mature very quickly.

'Torie, dear, you didn't need to do that,' Tiger-nanny reproved him quietly, but underneath her grey coat her tail twitched a little with annoyance and concern. 'Now you've upset him, you see.'

'He upsets *me*,' said Salvatore in a very grown-up voice. 'And he's *not* my brother!'

'Oh, shut him up, for the love of Mike!' said Julius, springing to the corridor side of the open compartment and blocking them all from the stares of the passengers. 'Give him a sweet or something, Nanny.'

Tiger-nanny whipped out a bottle and gave it to Samantha. 'Feed the baby, dear,' she said, and putting her paws round Salvatore she took him to the porthole corner of the cabin.

'Torie darling, you are quite right that the little baby is not your brother,' she whispered. 'We are taking him home to his own Mummy in Matsumundu. But it is a big secret, do you see? Just in case anybody else wants to get him first.'

'Yes,' said Salvatore, perfectly satisfied. 'Why didn't you say so before?'

'Are you all right, Nanny? Tell me when you want me to warm up baby's bottles. Shall I put your hat and coat up on the rack for you?' said the air hostess, suddenly appearing.

'No thank you, dear,' Tiger-nanny said hastily.

The hostess looked most incredulously at her woolly gloves, for although it was late in the year and cool outside, inside the cabin it was really very warm.

'Do you get chilblains?' she asked kindly.

'The palms of my hands are so rough,' said Tiger-nanny quickly. She could not bear to tell untruths in front of the children, but it was quite true, the pads beneath her paws were hard and rough, it was only the tops that were so soft and velvety, and striped so beautifully in gold and black.

'Oh, what a shame! I'll let you have some of my special handcream! I got it in Hong Kong,' the air hostess cried to Tiger-nanny's consternation, but at that moment the engines of the plane began to vibrate, the gangway was removed and the doors closed, while a moment later they were taxiing out on to the runway and the hostess ran to supervise the fastening and adjusting of seat belts among the passengers.

Not until they had left the ground and the city was a mere toy park below them did Tiger-nanny relax.

'And now I think we ought to have a very pleasant journey,' she said.

'Except that Salvatore is always sick all the time,' said Julius.

'Yes, I am,' said Salvatore.

'Oh, *no*! Somebody should have told me!' said Tiger-nanny in horror. 'I would have put his old blue jersey on.'

'But then the baby's mummy wouldn't have seen my new reefer coat,' said Salvatore rather loudly. When they all talked him down he realized what he had done, and buried his head, abashed, in Tiger-nanny's fur, hugging his blanket. He stayed there, looking pale, for the whole of the first part of the journey, and Tiger-nanny did not dare to move, for fear that Julius's prophecies came true.

There was one advantage: it kept the air hostess away. With the baby asleep on Samantha's lap and Salvatore on Tiger-nanny's she had only to wave a gloved paw and the hostess, looking understanding, took her tube of handcream elsewhere. By the time trays of lunch arrived the elder children, overcome by boredom, were sleeping too. And again Tiger-nanny waved her own tray aside. Nannies are all self-sacrificing and the hostess saw nothing strange in this behaviour.

Outside the porthole little wisps of cloud hid the land below, and presently a gap in the cloud showed Tiger-nanny that they were over the water, and there was no more land to be seen at all. She hoped it was not very deep water, and hugged Salvatore closer.

'I shan't be sick yet. I still feel quite nice inside,' he murmured.

They flew on and on. The cabin became intolerably warm but Tiger-nanny dared not even take her gloves off. They flew over more land which made her feel safer, and more sea, that made her feel nervous.

Julius woke and fetched iced drinks for them all but nobody wanted anything to eat. The baby prince had another bottle and then another. His thirst was prodigious. Tiger-nanny hoped they would have enough bottles to last him all the flight, but she had heard that they kept baby food on the plane.

The air hostess seemed to be kept busy looking after the needs of the other passengers and only looked in now and then to ask if they were all right.

Tiger-nanny told them all stories and Salvatore was not sick.

'He soon will be though,' said Julius.

'Yes,' said Salvatore, 'but please tell us the story first about the naughty little children who came to the Zoological Gardens.'

They had come to the very end of the story when a loud voice somewhere in the middle of the plane announced:

'Keep calm, please! This is a hold-up! I have got all the passengers covered, Captain! I have reason to believe that the heir to Matsumundu is travelling incognito on this flight. I represent the Free Party of Matsumundu who are determined to see their country liberated from unjust restrictions imposed on us by the present ruler and his heirs. Will you please fly the plane straight to Haifan in the province of Tulu-Zonga, where the Free Matsumundu Party is forming a government?'

Nobody spoke, but a kind of shudder went through

the plane, which continued on its course as if the hi-jacker had not spoken.

'Captain, I am waiting!' came the threatening voice. 'I have the passengers covered with my revolver. And I have the little prince a hostage in the back cabin entirely in my power. Should anything happen to him, Captain, it will be entirely your responsibility.'

Slowly, reluctantly, the passengers saw a wing dip to the right as the plane altered course.

'Shall I tackle him?' Julius whispered, half rising from his seat.

'No, no, *no*!' said Tiger-nanny, holding him down with one paw. 'Wait, dear, wait. If the plane crashes and everyone is killed it won't help anybody.'

A crackling, roaring noise came through the amplifier.

'The pilot says he hasn't got enough fuel to fly to Tulu-Zonga,' said one passenger to another.

Tiger-nanny could see the hi-jacker now, when she craned her neck sideways. He was quite an ordinary looking person, but she remembered seeing him come up the gangway because his handkerchief was dirty. He was standing in the gangway now with a revolver in his hand, sweeping the barrel from left to right as if to cover every passenger and hostess in the cabin.

'If anybody leaves their seat I shall shoot,' he announced.

'But, sir, the pilot hasn't got enough petrol to take

the plane to Tulu-Zonga,' said the air hostess nearest to him.

'Ha! I've heard that story before!' said the hi-jacker harshly.

Another protest came over the loudspeaker.

'It's quite true! You'll ditch the lot of us!' shouted a passenger. 'Put your gun away, man, there's no harm done so far. Nobody is going to tell on you if you give up now!'

The hi-jacker turned on him.

'Any more remarks from anybody else and I shall shoot at once,' he said, turning his gun on the speaker, who subsided hastily rather than stare into the wicked-looking barrel of the revolver.

'We'll take a chance on the petrol!' the hi-jacker said. 'I guess the pilot is just having his little game with us.'

'What's the matter?' said Salvatore, sitting up suddenly. 'Can we have our lunch now?'

'Not just yet, dear, I'll find you some boiled sweets,' said Tiger-nanny. Samantha was crying quietly in a corner, as she fed a fifth bottle to the baby prince.

Julius was sitting up very straight and serious with his clenched hands in his pockets trying to think of a rescue project. He had dreamt so often of rescuing and taking over a plane threatened by hi-jackers but now that it was happening no practical idea seemed to come into his head.

'Does he want to take away our baby?' said Salvatore. 'Well, we won't let him, will we?'

'No dear!' said Tiger-nanny, kissing the top of his head.

They flew on and on, and presently Tiger-nanny saw that the hi-jacker was slowly edging himself backwards towards their rear compartment.

At the same time a distinct undertone of murmuring could be heard among the passengers who were talking under their breaths but with an atmosphere of determination and purposefulness that could hardly deceive anyone travelling in the aircraft.

The hi-jacker shouted to them to stop talking, but although their lips were closed the murmuring went on.

The pilot called back that the petrol was getting low, and this time the hi-jacker seemed to believe him.

'Can you put down at Beebo?' he asked.

'Beebo is further away than Tulu-Zonga!' the pilot buzzed back.

'Then fly right on!' ordered the hi-jacker. The passengers stopped murmuring under their breaths, pulled out their survival instruction leaflets and began to read them.

Tiger-nanny too made her little preparations: she wrapped an inflatable life-jacket round the little prince and another round Salvatore, inflated both and showed the other children what to do with theirs when and if they got into the water.

'Cor, Sally and the baby look just like puddings,' said Julius. 'I shall eat you, Sally, only I know you will taste disgusting.'

'I shan't!' said Salvatore angrily. 'Don't call me Sally.'

'I'd rather eat a frog,' said Julius, looking at him critically. 'Actually I don't think I'd touch you if I hadn't had anything to eat for a fortnight.'

'Tiger-nanny, put your life-jacket on!' Samantha urged her. 'I believe we are going lower.'

'Let's put Baby into his cot, he'll float longer, and, Julius, don't let go of Salvatore!' Tiger-nanny said.

'Come here, pudding!' said Julius.

Salvatore and Julius were having a pitched battle with fists, and Tiger-nanny, rather perplexed, had shed her hat, coat, gloves and was about to put on her life-jacket when the pilot's laconic order 'Prepare to ditch!' came over the loudspeaker and the engines ceased vibrating. The plane was heading in a long, quiet dive towards the sea.

'There's a raft between the seats, Nanny. If I can't get to you, push it out of the doors by the gangway. You'll be the first out with the children!' the air hostess called back to them.

'Don't move, please, anybody until I say so!' cried the hi-jacker. 'Nobody is to leave their seats until I have got clear of the plane.'

His voice grew louder and nearer as he came backwards down the plane towards them, and the next moment he had retreated into their compartment and was standing in the entrance with his back to them, still sweeping the barrel of his revolver backwards and forwards across the ranks of terrified passengers in the body of the plane.

'Steward!' he called. 'Come up here and stand beside me. When the plane lands on the water, drop out the life-raft in the nursery compartment and push it through the doors. Nanny! You there behind me with the children! Hand me the baby the moment I tell you to do so. Have you put him in his life-saving jacket?'

'Yes I have,' snapped Tiger-nanny. 'But you aren't taking him out on the sea in that outfit. He must go in his cot.'

'I'll be the judge of that!' said the hi-jacker tartly over his shoulder.

'Don't let the dirty man have him!' wailed Salvatore.

'Look here! You buzz off!' Julius ordered the hi-jacker with trembling knees.

'You horrible, horrible man!' shrieked Samantha hysterically.

'Be quiet, all of you!' ordered Tiger-nanny.

'Kids will be kids!' said the hi-jacker, without looking round. 'All right, Nanny, I'm not going to hurt *your* lot. Just put the baby under my left arm – now! Because if you don't, Nanny, I'm going to turn round and put a bullet right through you in exactly half a minute, see?'

For answer there came the most ear-splitting roar. The passengers thought the plane had hit the water and was breaking into pieces. But the noise went on and increased in volume to a tremendous crescendo as Tiger-nanny leaped out of her seat, trumpeting with the full power of all her jungle ancestors as she launched herself at the hi-jacker's back.

He heard her coming and half turned round, an incredulous expression spreading over his face and his eyes starting out of his head. But it was too late to shoot. With the whole force of her body and claws Tiger-nanny knocked him to the ground, crunching the remains of the revolver in her teeth as she sat with her full weight upon his unconscious body.

In the terror of this unexpected and dramatic encounter the screaming passengers hardly noticed that the pilot had put down the plane quite smoothly on to a calm though swift-running sea, where it bobbed cheerfully like a baby's toy on the sunbright surface.

A steward dashed to open the plane doors next to the children's compartment. Since he had to step right across the hi-jacker and brush past the well-grown tiger cat sitting on his prostrate body, this was probably the bravest thing he ever did in his life, but the steward had no thought for his own safety at this moment. Julius helped to drag out the raft and let it into the sea, secured by a little rope. He helped his sister and Salvatore to drop into it and clambered down to receive the little prince, but Tiger-nanny jumped lightly after him with the handles of the travelling-cot fast in her jaws.

'Anyone else coming on this raft?' the steward called. 'There are plenty of others. Keep calm. There is no immediate danger.'

The passengers hesitated and held back. Nobody wanted to go on the raft with the children and Tiger-nanny. Julius released the cord that held it to the doorway and the current swiftly whisked the raft away from the aircraft's side.

Now the passengers began to clamber out of every available entrance and to sit along the wings and structure like swallows preparing for their winter flight. The children could see the crew leaving their cabin and struggling along the plane to help the passengers. Last of all, the hi-jacker was handed out, trussed up like a chicken, ready to be put on the last raft with the crew. Everyone seemed in good spirits and there was plenty of room. The weather was fine and there did not seem to be any immediate danger of the aeroplane sinking.

'I expect the captain has radioed for help,' Tiger-nanny said. 'It will not be difficult to find such a big target in the sea. I think we had better go back and wait with the others.'

But when Tiger-nanny and the children paddled alongside the wings none of the passengers was at all anxious to welcome their party.

'Give us the baby and the little boy!' they called, holding out kindly arms. 'And you come too, dearie, with your sister,' they said to Julius. 'But not the tiger.'

'Oh, pooh to you!' said Julius rudely.

The pilot shouted across the fuselage. 'Don't bring that tiger up here – not on any account! You had no business to bring it on board.'

'If we hadn't brought Tiger-nanny some of you would have been shot dead!' Julius yelled back.

'She's our Tiger-nanny, not a tiger!' shouted Samantha.

'You are awful people!' yelled Salvatore.

'Sorry, kids, but you just can't bring her with you!' said the captain more reasonably, preparing to lift them aboard. 'Her claws for one thing. Any rip in this fuselage and we'll all go to the bottom as sure as God made little apples.'

'And God made tigers too!' sobbed Salvatore. 'I *won't* go without Tiger-nanny.'

'I won't either,' said Julius and Samantha.

'Well, hand us up the baby. He seems to be the cause of all the trouble!' said the captain.

'Excuse me, sir, but the baby is in my charge,' said Tiger-nanny stiffly. 'Where he goes, I go with him.'

'Come on, let's leave these parasites!' said Julius, fishing for a derogatory word and paddling the little raft out of reach of the captain standing on the wing.

'To tell you the truth, my dears, I feel we are much

safer by ourselves in the raft,' said Tiger-nanny. 'All those people sitting along the fabric, it looks very risky to me. I am sure the rescue aircraft will pick us up quite quickly if we don't move very far away.'

But it was more easily said than done.

The strong current took the little raft in tow, and although they all paddled against it in turn it was much too strong for them to resist. The aircraft became a smaller and smaller object behind them.

At first the passengers sang and waved, then the sound of their singing fell away and their waving handkerchiefs were swallowed up in the breasting swell of the great waves that swept the raft up, up, up and shot it down, down, down again on the deceptively calm surface of the sea.

'I have never not been seasick for so long in my life before,' said Salvatore proudly.

'You are a very clever little boy,' said Tiger-nanny kindly.

'And I have left my Fluff behind on the aeroplane,' said Salvatore with less confidence.

'You are a very *brave* little boy!' said Tiger-nanny.

'And I'm thirsty and my head aches and I feel awful!' said Salvatore, bursting into tears just as the baby, who had been asleep all the time, woke up and began to bawl for another bottle. Samantha dealt with him while Tiger-nanny comforted Salvatore.

'Don't give him all of it, dear!' she warned Samantha. 'We only have three prepared bottles left in the case. And I do think Torie could have a little drink now.'

'Not out of a bottle!' protested Salvatore, but he took it all the same.

'We shall surely get picked up before dark!' thought Tiger-nanny, calculating the time in bottles.

But they were not.

Darkness fell with great rapidity and they had lost sight of the aircraft long ago.

They had no means of attracting attention to themselves in the night. Julius had discovered a flare in the raft but in wrangling over it with Salvatore, who thought it might be something to eat, they had dropped it overboard between them. They were all ravenously hungry, including, it seemed, the little prince who had at least had his regular meals all day long, with one or two over. But even Salvatore agreed it seemed terrible to rob a baby, and lay, hungry and blanketless, with his head in Tiger-nanny's flanks, pretending that her tail was his Fluff.

Soon after nightfall Tiger-nanny heard the hum of an approaching aeroplane. The children were asleep, but on a forlorn hope she nudged Julius gently in the ribs.

'I suppose you didn't bring your torch with you, did you, love?' she whispered.

'Oh blast, no!' he murmured, half asleep. Five minutes later, when the plane was out of hearing, he woke up with a start. 'Oh, I dreamt I had it under my pillow!' he exclaimed. 'But I haven't got a pillow, have I? Sorry, Tiger-nanny!'

Tiger-nanny licked his ear gently until he was once more sleeping soundly. She hoped the baby would sleep until daylight too and not wake all the others by clamouring for a bottle in the middle of the night.

8 · *Landfall*

Tiger-nanny stayed awake for half the night and then she too slept, worn out by anxiety and the rocking of the sea.

Like Julius she had hopeful dreams. She dreamed she was back in the park, pushing a pram, with Salvatore on his tricycle beside her and the other children teasing her to buy them ice-creams. She dreamt she had sent them off to fetch some and had gone to sit underneath a shady tree with the baby, rocking the pram gently to and fro with the end of her tail. She thought it was very pleasant in the park this afternoon. Such a nice sunny day . . .

When she woke up she found it really was a nice sunny day, but she was not sitting in the park. She was not sailing on the sea either. The boat had drifted on to a shore with the whitest of sands, and palm trees in the background. There were huts, too, though of such a tumbledown appearance that at first she took them for chicken houses, but the scrawny chickens pecking round the walls did not seem to live in any houses at all.

Tiger-nanny looked immediately to see whether

the baby was awake inside the travelling cot, but to her horror she saw that the cot was empty. Although she had not opened her eyes longer than a few seconds it seemed a lifetime while she realized that none of the children was with her in the boat.

They were, in fact, standing a little distance off, on the white sands of the shore, talking to a handful of ragged people.

Samantha had the baby in her arms and was showing it off with possessive pride and pleasure.

The people were dressed in poor and faded garments, while the children ran half naked, but one and all were so engrossed in the baby and in examining it all over that they did not notice Tiger-nanny's sudden leap out of the boat, nor hear her anxious footfalls padding up the beach, as she hurried to the children's side, an indignant growl rising in her throat.

'Hullo, Tiger-nanny!' said Salvatore.

The island inhabitants fell away with shrieks of terror. Tiger-nanny snatched the baby from Samantha's arms with little ceremony and carried him squalling back to the boat.

The inhabitants fled back to their houses wailing desperately. They quite evidently thought that the baby was going to be eaten by the tiger. Since they all consisted of women and children it was hardly surprising that they now dived inside their derelict shacks to summon help from their husbands who came out dishevelled with sleep, loading their guns.

Tiger-nanny and the children watched from the boat, the little prince held securely between Tiger-nanny's paws, soothed by the familiar kindness of her fur. The inhabitants had skin the same olive tint as the baby's. Their hair was oily and dark. But far more disturbing to Tiger-nanny was the likeness between them and the late hi-jacker on the aeroplane, who had worn, she remembered immediately, a narrow yellow and red ribbon tied round his left wrist identical to those worn by these people. On the same wrist the little prince wore a gold-sealed wristlet like a snake. It was, Tiger-nanny had told Julius, the sign of his royal birth, and in England she had been very careful to keep it tucked away under the sleeve of his woolly coat.

But on the sea his little arms had been unprotected, he had kicked and waved as he pleased. The ragged women had fingered and investigated the golden token as Samantha held the baby in her arms.

'I think they know who he is,' she confessed to Tiger-nanny. 'I'm very sorry. I didn't think about it mattering in a place like this.'

But it did matter, that was evident. The men advanced in a menacing line, aiming at Tiger-nanny with their rifles. One or two waded into the sea to get a better sighting that would not endanger the children, but they all flung themselves upon her, clinging to her sides and neck.

'It's OK, kiddy! We don't shoot you – only the tiger!' one of the men announced. His voice was not at all English which made it much more frightening in the present circumstances.

'No! No! No!' they shouted. 'Not Tiger-nanny! Don't shoot Tiger-nanny!'

The men had no chance to shoot while Julius, Samantha and Salvatore clung so desperately to her. They lowered their guns.

'Look, missy!' one of them called to Samantha. 'You give us baby and we don't shoot nobody – see?'

'I will *not!*' said Samantha with dignity and courage.

'That's my good girl,' said Tiger-nanny.

'Do tiger bite?' another man said, wading closer to the boat. Tiger-nanny growled very threateningly.

'Yes,' said Julius. 'It will bite *you!*'

'It eats people whole!' shrieked Salvatore from somewhere under Tiger-nanny's armpit. 'It has eaten lots and lots of people – *all up*!'

'Torie, darling, that isn't true,' Tiger-nanny scolded in an undertone. 'And it is very rude and very naughty to say such things. You know it is.'

'I'm sorry, Tiger-nanny!' Salvatore rumbled. 'But you will eat them up if they shoot us, won't you, Tiger-nanny?'

'They won't shoot us,' said Tiger-nanny decidedly. 'Sit up and behave like a big boy. There is nothing to be afraid of.'

In fact the men were wading out of the sea and those on the shore had dropped their rifles to their sides and were standing in little groups, discussing matters.

Tiger-nanny wondered whether they could not between them push the raft back into the sea and leave the place, but the sun was becoming increasingly hot, and they had no fresh water and hardly any milk. Neither had they any food at all.

As if he read her thoughts, one of the men came a step closer and announced:

'You can't leave this place. By noonday the sun will be so hot in the sky you will all be roasted dead out there in the water. We know who that baby is. He belong to our country of Matsumundu, not to yours. We tell his mum and dadda about him. We give you a nice house to live in and good food and drinks till his mumma and dadda come along.'

There did not seem to be any alternative, and already the men seemed a little more friendly. The children left the raft first, and then, clinging close to Tiger-nanny, who carried the baby in the travelling-cot, they followed the men up the shore to one of the dark, squalid houses overlooking the sea.

It was so dark inside that it took a little while to discover that it consisted of one large room only, with a primitive cooking stove in one corner, a barred window, some dirty mattresses and a couple of cooking pots and drinking vessels.

'How nasty!' said Samantha.

'Shut up!' said Julius ominously. She looked where he was looking, and saw that a couple of men with rifles had taken up positions just outside the door. Samantha jumped back.

'One thing, they'll never try to shoot Tiger-nanny inside here,' Julius said, to comfort Samantha who had begun to sob. 'They'd hit the baby for sure.'

They huddled round Tiger-nanny who was trying to pacify the hungry baby. To her dismay she found that the last milk remaining to them had gone sour.

While she nursed and comforted him a jug of milk and some rolls, fruit and cheese were pushed through the door and soon the baby's howls were quenched. He had no objection, it seemed, to substituting goats' milk for the expensive preparations he had been fed on in England, and long before the rest of them had finished what Julius rudely called 'a filthy meal', he was fast asleep.

It grew hotter and hotter. From time to time their water jug was refilled, while meat and vegetables of an exceedingly poor quality were brought in a basket at midday. As it was raw, Tiger-nanny had to cook it for them on the stove, which made it taste worse, rather than better, Julius said. 'Not that I blame your cooking, Tiger-nanny,' he added. 'Nobody could make food like that taste nice.'

'Then just eat what you can and leave the rest, dear,' said Tiger-nanny. 'Remember, there are lots of little children starving in some parts of the world who would be thankful for what is left on the sides of people's plates.'

'We *are* those little children!' said Samantha gloomily, remembering overloaded dishes at hotels, while dining out with her mother and Lucien. 'Oh, Ju, wouldn't you just *love* an ice-cream!'

Salvatore began to cry.

'The first thing you shall have when we get back to Mummy and Daddy is a *big* ice-cream!' said Tiger-nanny, consoling him. 'What will be your first thing, Julius?'

'A double brandy,' said Julius, imitating his

stepfather's voice. Tiger-nanny boxed his ears, but not very hard.

'And I shall put on some of Mummy's perfume,' said Samantha. 'This place smells vile! – I mean lovely!' she added hastily as one of the guards happened to glance in their direction.

Salvatore still sobbed.

'Be a brave boy!' Tiger-nanny urged him. 'It won't be very long and then you shall have your nice ice-cream.'

'I don't want an ice-cream!' Salvatore sobbed. 'I'm thinking about Fluff being drowned in that aeroplane!'

'Oh, *Fluff!*' said Julius in disgust.

'I don't think he has been drowned!' Tiger-nanny purred. 'I believe . . .' and she began a long story about the possible rescue of Fluff by sea-horses, mermaids, pirates, his adventures and hairbreadth escapes until he reached Salvatore's arms again. Salvatore fell asleep long before the end.

9 · *The captain*

Not all of them could use Tiger-nanny for a pillow, and when they did her fur was very hot to lie upon, but the alternative was the dirty mattresses in the corner, so they tried. She herself had to sit fairly upright to shield the baby without suffocating him, and to keep watch on the guards and as much as she could see through the open door.

The village was extremely primitive but it had its civilized pretensions. Two or three bicycles clattered by on what appeared to be the rims of their wheels, and at some time during the morning an ear-splitting roar sounded as if some vintage motorcycle were being launched as a space rocket. Its agonies died away in the distance. It was the only engine they ever heard in the village, but once or twice the shrill ringing of a telephone bell sounded, as if the inhabitants had some kind of communication with a wider world. Tiger-nanny was glad to know this. She thought it meant an earlier liberation, which was a relief, because she did not like these people at all, especially the men.

She listened to the guards talking while the children slept, but they spoke their own language and she could not understand it at all.

Presently she was aware that Julius was awake and listening too. He had travelled so much with his mother that he had picked up quite a number of languages.

'Do you understand what they are saying?' she murmured into his ear.

'Sort of,' he answered, and a little later: 'I can't tell you now, but later, when the baby cries again, let him roar a bit and put your ear very close to my mouth, then I'll tell you!'

It was easier because the little prince became hungry before fresh milk rations arrived. Perhaps the goats were only milked twice a day. The guards looked in and made gestures that supplies were on the way but as the cries became louder and louder they shrugged their shoulders helplessly and finally sat down with their hands over their ears to shut out the pitiful sounds.

Julius put his lips to Tiger-nanny's ear.

'They were talking about their leader,' he murmured. 'They call him the captain. They've sent for *him*, not for the baby's parents at all. They're all rebels, like the hi-jacker was. He was one of their men.'

'But the rebellion is over!' Samantha said, sitting up beside him. 'There's nothing left to have a revolution about! They're going to have their cinemas and their films, and now they've got Mummy coming to make one right in their own country, what more do they want?'

The baby's screams covered their conversation so that Julius was able to relax a little and answer her.

'That's just it!' he said in some excitement. 'This captain of theirs, he wants to corner it all! He wants to own the whole state cinema concern and get all the profits! If he captures the baby they think he will be able to exchange him for a contract giving him all the rights – over Lucien's film and everything! Well, it doesn't matter much to us. I expect Mum will get the money just the same!'

'Julius, that isn't the way to talk!' said Tiger-nanny, giving the screaming baby a little pat. '(There, there! Milky's coming!) Just think of the poor, poor baby in the care of these people and of his poor mummy and daddy's feelings while he is being held to ransom. You mustn't be selfish, you know.'

'I know!' Julius agreed reluctantly. 'Oh, thank God, here comes the milk! There's some of his sufferings over, anyway. I say,. Tiger-nanny, you don't think they are going to make us sleep in this dump, do you?'

But they were.

Night fell suddenly. The guards were changed, the last food supplies and a pitcher of milk were thrust through the doorway. The day was over, and a long, long spell of darkness divided them from the next.

They were settling down to an uneasy sleep, when footsteps came striding along the beach, torches flared, the guards sprang to attention, and the shadow of a tall figure, crowned by a battered felt hat, suddenly loomed across them from the open doorway.

They did not need telling that this was the captain the guards had been talking about. He had every appearance of a rebel leader, even to the cartridge belt slung about his waist. His long shaggy hair and rough beard suggested that he had been living out for several days, and even without the menace of Tiger-nanny's growling he seemed unwilling to come inside four walls.

'Give me that child!' he ordered Julius, holding out a hand that had seen every other duty except washing.

Julius was silent. The man was dominating, arrogant, almost compelling, but he knew that Tiger-nanny was stronger still. She snarled, half waking Salvatore who murmured 'Fluff' and clutched her tail again.

The captain conferred with his guards. They pointed at Tiger-nanny, made signs and gestures, and finally shrugged their shoulders helplessly.

'Very well then, Mandoline Harper's children! You come with me! You shall telephone to your mother and tell her where you are!' the captain said, looking at Julius through narrowed eyes.

Samantha sprang joyfully forward but Tiger-nanny clawed her back again. 'Not one of you leaves my side!' she muttered fiercely. Samantha looked deeply disappointed but obeyed.

'Silly fool!' Julius hissed at her. 'He didn't mean it!'

The captain glared at them, then withdrew. A little later one of the guards arrived with a large meat bone that he threw on the ground for Tiger-nanny.

The children were asleep again. Tiger-nanny had eaten very little all day, and the smell of the meat made her whiskers twitch with hunger and excitement. She had learned to eat English food, even English nursery food, as befitted her profession, but her mind did stray occasionally to the delicious meals the keeper had given her in the Zoological Gardens, meals designed with tigers only in mind, and nothing at all to do with the bringing up of children. It was the first time since she left home that anyone had offered her a bone, and it looked delicious.

Careful not to disturb the children she stretched out a paw and pulled the bone towards her, sniffing and nuzzling it while her mouth watered. Biting and chewing it would disturb her charges, but she could just lick at it while they slept. Even to know that it was there consoled her.

Then she saw one of the guards squinting at her sideways through the door. She growled very quietly to show him that she knew he was there, and all of a sudden she knew why he was looking at *her* and not at the children. He wanted to watch her eating her bone!

Why?

At once Tiger-nanny knew why, even before, with the tip of her tongue, she had tasted the strange sweetish flavour on the bone that was not entirely the flavour of meat. The bone was poisoned! Very quietly but firmly she rolled it away so that it landed in a dark corner where the children would not touch it by accident. That the captain had intended it for her alone she knew well – but little Torie might get some on his fingers.

She was anxious now, very anxious, not for herself, but for what would happen to the children if any harm came to her. Not a wink of sleep did she allow herself until the dawn came, although the guards dozed outside and none of the children so much as stirred in their dreaming.

Food arrived with morning light and the guards were replaced. Again Julius listened to their conversation.

'What happened to you last night?' he whispered into Tiger-nanny's ear under cover of the baby's hungry bawling. 'They say you ate a bone that was meant to get rid of you for good!'

'I didn't eat the bone,' said Tiger-nanny with dignity. 'And I want you to dig a hole in the corner of the hut, kick it in with your paw – I mean your foot – and bury it. And then come straight back to me.'

Julius did as he was told, but while he was digging and Tiger-nanny was feeding the baby, someone climbed very quietly up the roof above their heads and removed a tile. Nobody could have fired a gun from this position without hurting most of the children as well as Tiger-nanny, but there are darts made to put wild animals to sleep and these cause very little noise or explosion when they are fired.

'Ping!' A sharp sting behind the ear made Tiger-nanny jump. She looked about her to swat at the wasp with her paw before it stung one of the children, but her paw felt so heavy she could scarcely lift it. The other paw was heavier still.

All over her body the feeling of heaviness spread. A sensation of deep lethargy began to creep over her. 'Of course, I never slept a wink all night,' she told herself. 'I'll just finish the baby's bottle and then I'll tell Julius to keep guard while I take a nap.'

But before Julius had returned from digging his hole Tiger-nanny's limbs had sagged and relaxed, her head had fallen forward across the little prince who lay contentedly sucking his bottle between her paws, and Tiger-nanny was fast asleep.

10 · *Capture of the children*

'She's tired,' said Julius, looking down at her.

'No she isn't,' said Salvatore.

'I don't wonder!' said Samantha. 'I bet she didn't sleep much last night. She was taking care of us all night long.'

'Tiger-nanny!' Salvatore said, pulling at her fur.

'Stop it, you silly little nit. Let her sleep and the baby too. He's stuffed full for a bit and we may get some peace for a while.' Julius turned to look out of the doorway and found that three soldiers were looking inside.

'Get out!' he ordered.

Instead, they took two or three steps inside the hut, watching Tiger-nanny very carefully.

'You get right outside at once!' said Julius fiercely. 'She'll have you if you don't! Hi! Tiger-nanny! They're coming in!'

The soldiers came in. They stood in a small group looking down at the sleeping tiger, her head across the baby's chest, her paws clasped lovingly about its body.

One of the men went back to the door and signalled to someone further away. At once a telephone started shrilling, then footsteps came in their direction and the captain stood in the entrance with a calculated smile upon his face. He took in the situation at a glance.

'You go over to the house there!' he told Julius, Samantha and Salvatore. 'Your momma and dadda are telephoning for you. You go and say you are safe.'

'How do you know it is them telephoning?' Julius said as the phone shrilled on.

'I put a call through first,' the captain grinned. None of the children believed him.

Samantha was shoving Tiger-nanny with her foot to wake her, but there was no response. Her striped sides heaved up and down in peaceful slumber. Her eyes were fast closed. Samantha felt terribly uneasy. It was so unlike Tiger-nanny to sleep through any kind of disturbance or danger. And then she saw the tiny dart sticking out behind the ear. She tried to snatch it away, but one of the soldiers stopped her.

'It's too late now!' the captain said, mocking her. 'Come along. The less fuss the better. Bring the baby, you fellows.'

Two of the soldiers stooped to remove the baby, with some reluctance and evident fear. Their nervousness was justified, for without waking Tiger-nanny let out a throaty roar that sent them jumping back so violently they cannoned into the captain. At the same moment Tiger-nanny tightened her grasp on the sleeping prince who was now gripped so firmly against her chest that it would have taken a mechanical grab to dislodge him.

'You get him!' the captain ordered Julius, who simply looked away, as if such an order were beneath his contempt.

'Then you do!' the captain said to Samantha, so fiercely that she was unnerved. She knelt beside the baby and actually put her arms round as much of him as she could gather, but finding himself being used as a kind of Christmas cracker with a rival pulling him at both ends, he woke up and began to yell. Tiger-nanny made a tremendous effort and half woke up. Once again the throaty snarl filled the hut, curdling everybody's blood. Then she made a half turn that enveloped the child almost completely underneath her body, and sank again into unconsciousness.

'Get them out of here!' the captain said to the soldiers.

They pushed the three elder children in front of them along the white beach, under the curious gaze of all the mothers and children who had welcomed them the day before. Then they turned inland towards a hut standing all by itself at the edge of the jungle-like forest.

Into the hut they pushed the children, and spent the rest of the day digging a deep pit all round it so that they could not get away.

The pit was covered with branches as if the captain suspected that Tiger-nanny would come hunting for the children the moment she was awake. At one point only a log of wood bridged the pit so that a guard could walk across to bring food and water at meal times. A soldier sat on guard with his gun on his knees and his eyes fixed on the hut where Tiger-nanny lay sleeping.

There was no window in the children's hut so they could not see what was going on outside. They sat and played all the games they knew that could be played in semi-darkness inside a hut. Nobody cried. While Tiger-nanny was alive – and she was alive – they trusted her to take them safely back to their parents. It was just a question of waiting. Even Salvatore did not grizzle, but nuzzled at a piece of moss and wished it smelt a little more like Fluff.

At three o'clock in the afternoon a hush fell on the village even greater than the usual quiet of the afternoon siesta.

The children felt it as they drowsed in the heat. Outside the hut they heard a click as the sentry cocked his gun.

'I bet it's Tiger-nanny!' Julius said, trembling with excitement.

'I can *feel* her coming!' said Salvatore.

'Oh, I do hope not!' Samantha said, clasping and unclasping her hands. 'Because if she comes out-of-doors they will be sure to shoot her!'

But it was not as easy to shoot or capture Tiger-nanny as the captain had expected.

She emerged from the hut looking to right and left with the baby in its travelling-cot dangling from her jaws. He had had his midday feed and was hiccuping joyously.

At once the men encircled her, keeping their distance and trying to aim where they would not risk hurting the baby, but it was almost impossible.

Even from the back Tiger-nanny kept turning her head from side to side and each time she turned it the baby's basket swung into view and became part of the target. If she were merely wounded and leapt into the air the little prince might be dropped and killed. It was much more important to keep the baby alive than to have Tiger-nanny dead.

'I think she's coming now,' said Salvatore.

'Let's shout, just in case she is, to show her where we are!' said Samantha.

They all shouted, 'Tiger-nanny! Tiger-nanny!'

There was a fierce expostulation from the sentry at the other side of the pit, but he was more worried about his own predicament than anything the children might do. The captain had told him to stay there, if the tiger approached the hut, until the very last possible moment. If he could shoot her first, well and good, but if he happened to miss her or anything went wrong he was to jump aside only at the very last instant and let Tiger-nanny go crashing through the boughs into the pit below. Nobody expected her to be carrying the baby at that stage, but everybody knew just what would be the fate of the person who allowed the little prince to come to harm.

So when the guard realized that the bundle in Tiger-nanny's mouth was the royal heir whose

pussy cross then? We'll put her in a cage and exhibit her when we open the Great Cinema Chain in Matsumundu! Pussy – Puss! Puss!'

Something creaked under the wall beside the door post. It was the end of a log that had been jammed there to hold it fast.

'He's standing on it!' Julius said. 'He's standing on the plank on top of the pit and Tiger-nanny is down below. Shall we tip him in?'

'Oh, poor Tiger-nanny. She'll be squashed!' said Samantha.

'No she won't!' said Salvatore.

'Come on!' said Julius giggling. 'Don't move it till I say. Put your hands here, Sammy, and you, Sal, here, on top of mine. When I say *Push!* shove with all your might!'

They knelt on the floor. Julius, for greater purchase, lay flat on his stomach with his head flat against the earth.

'Ready?' he muttered. 'One – two – three – *Push!*'

The end of the log shot out beyond the wall. There came a crash as it thundered into the pit, and a much louder crash accompanied by oaths as the captain thundered down after it.

Julius tugged at the door which opened in his hands. There had been no need for locks with the pit and an armed guard outside.

All three children crouched on the sill, staring down into the pit, while on the farther side the men huddled open-mouthed and horrified, expecting to see their leader torn to pieces under their eyes.

Even Julius, Samantha and Salvatore expected that Tiger-nanny would take some action, pinning him down with her paws perhaps or just giving him a swipe that would send him head over heels into another part of the pit, but she did nothing of the kind. She merely removed his gun and sat on it, well out of reach of the baby, who was tucked away behind her now, gazing up at the gaping soldiers and laughing at them.

Tiger-nanny sat upright on her haunches. The captain seemed to shrink as she stared at him. He cowered away, waiting for her to strike.

'You *dirty* man!' Tiger-nanny said, lashing her tail ever so slightly. 'Blow your nose!'

The captain hastily wiped his face with the back of his hand.

'*Not* that way!' said Tiger-nanny. 'Here! Have a tissue!'

She deftly flicked a tissue from the baby's travelling-cot and waited while he used it. A murmur of amusement went round the watching gallery above. They had never seen their leader use a tissue before.

The captain flushed angrily and threw the tissue to the ground.

'Pick it up and put it in your pocket!' said Tiger-nanny calmly. 'You can find a waste-paper basket when you get home.'

Sulkily he thrust the tissue into his trousers.

'Just *look* at your hands!' Tiger-nanny continued. 'Don't tell me you don't bite your nails because I shan't believe it. And your *shirt*! Little Salvatore makes less mess of his meals than you do and he is dirty for his age. I haven't got a sponge down here but we can at least clean you up a bit.'

To the terror of the rebel captain she took his ears in her paws, tilted his head to one side and began to wash his face and neck with her large pink tongue. Salvatore, who had also suffered such indignities, shrieked with joy, but the soldiers looked anxious. When, however, they saw Tiger-nanny drying the captain with the baby's spare nappy and powdering his ears with talc their relief was so excessive that they broke into guffaws of laughter that echoed round and round the pit, to the great discomfiture of their leader.

He was left sitting with the nappy knotted at the back of his neck, like a bib, and his fingers stuffed into the baby's mittens.

'That will teach you not to bite your nails,' Tiger-nanny told him.

The three children were rolling about with joy, while the men, having thrown down their guns, were summoning their families to come and watch the exquisite entertainment of their leader's discomfiture. All their fear, all their respect for him had suddenly vanished. His leadership had evaporated under the discipline of Tiger-nanny's warm pink tongue.

The men laid the log across the pit and the three children ran across to freedom.

'What happens now?' asked Samantha.

'Get on that telephone!' Julius ordered one of the men. 'Ring up the palace and tell the king that we are all here and his baby is safe and we need a car sent for us. And tell him to get in touch with Mandy and Lucien and say we aren't drowned or anything. They'll want to be getting on making the film.'

'But what about our cinema?' the men asked, hesitating.

'You're *getting* your cinema – idiots!' Julius

exploded. 'How could you possibly trust a man like that? If he cornered it it would be because he wanted all the profits and in next to no time you'd find all the prices going up and you couldn't afford to go and take your children. Now, my mum and stepfather are here to make a perfectly splendid film in your own country and I'll see you all get free tickets for the opening night. Only get that baby back to his parents and us back to ours, so they can get going on it. Because if I know Mandy she'll be having hysterics from morning till night if she thinks we are dead.'

'But the tiger?' they asked anxiously.

'That's not a tiger, that's our nanny!' said Julius. 'You can see she wouldn't hurt a fly. Not if the fly didn't hurt us, that's to say.'

Somebody was sent to fetch a ladder.

'But – him?' the men persisted, pointing at their one-time leader.

'Leave him down there to cool off,' Julius suggested. 'If he's hungry he can have the baby's dummy to suck.'

Tiger-nanny emerged from the pit with the dignity of the Queen of Sheba arriving to greet King Solomon. The three children flung themselves upon her.

The ex-captain did not even attempt to follow her up the ladder. He preferred to nurse his humiliation alone.

The entire village collected to pay homage to Tiger-nanny and the baby. Men, women and children ventured closer until they were actually stroking her fur, and everybody was careful to wash their hands before they did so.

The telephone in its primitive cabin shrieked incessantly. The palace demanded confirmation of the prince's safety, first from Julius and then from Tiger-nanny herself. Even then she would not let go of the baby's cot, but spoke, rather indistinctly, with the handles dangling from her chin.

Then it was Mandoline Harper calling for her children.

'Darlings! Darlings!' she moaned. 'Oh, my darlings, the strain has been killing me!'

'What? What? I can't hear what you are saying,' Julius said. 'You take her, Sammy, she's gone all creaky.'

'Mummy! We're all right! We're all *right*!' Samantha cried into the crackling instrument. 'Go on, Torie – you try!'

'Darlings! The STRAIN HAS BEEN KILLING ME!' Mandoline Harper bawled.

'No it hasn't,' said Salvatore. 'Good-bye, Mummy. Where's Daddy?'

'Torie, dear, that wasn't very polite,' said Tiger-nanny, but the line had gone dead.

'I hope they send a Bentley for us!' Julius said. 'That's what I really would enjoy. To drive out of this infernal village in a Bentley, or a helicopter of course.'

But it was neither a Bentley nor a helicopter that picked them up, it was a neat little motor-cruiser from the sea with several of the government troops on board. When they had welcomed the children and Tiger-nanny and received the baby like the lost headpiece of the crown jewels, they proceeded to the pit and hooked the rebel captain out like a stickleback out of a jam-jar. Still wearing his impromptu bib (the mittens had been ground into the floor of the pit), he was tied up and bundled into some remote compartment of the cabin-cruiser, where he remained perfectly invisible during the voyage up the coast to the capital.

The people of the village, having voluntarily surrendered their weapons, were so harangued by the leader of the government forces that even Tiger-nanny could not have done it better. As the cruiser put off from shore the children noticed that some of them were left in tears.

'I wonder how long it will take to build them a cinema,' said Samantha sympathetically.

12 · *Queen of the nursery*

Life at the king's palace was so utterly different from their recent experiences that the village soon faded out of their minds.

Used as they were at home to spoiling and unlimited attention, the children had never met quite so much indulgence and affection as they received from the king of Matsumundu, his wife and the entire staff of his palace. Mandoline Harper's fame paled beside the glory that surrounded Tiger-nanny, Julius, Samantha and Salvatore.

The baby prince lay in the centre of it all like a pearl in an oyster. Had it not been for Tiger-nanny's supervision he would have been ruined, to the inevitable downfall of his future kingdom, but she ruled the nursery, by the king's insistence, with a paw of iron, and the baby flourished.

The film progressed even better than Lucien had expected in spite of Mandoline's tantrums, but Julius, Samantha and Salvatore ran wild and became utterly impossible to control.

'This is the last time I take those kids on location,'

Lucien said firmly. 'When we get back to London they are all going to boarding-school.'

'Tiger-nanny will have to come back with us, so she can manage them in the holidays,' sniffed Mandoline. 'They'll kill me between them if she doesn't.'

The children heard the news with fury and despair. '*School!*' they raged. 'No more travelling! No more hi-jackers and bandits! And how can we possibly live without Tiger-nanny?'

'It's your own fault,' said Tiger-nanny crossly, knitting crawlers from an English pattern for the little prince. 'If you had not got upon your parents' nerves this would not have happened. You know perfectly well how to please them if you choose.'

'But we can't live without you, Tiger-nanny!' they wailed.

'Nonsense,' said Tiger-nanny. 'You are all quite old enough to go to school without a nanny. Why, even Torie goes to sleep without a Fluff these days.'

Tiger-nanny had a suite of nurseries to herself and little golden-skinned slaves to wait on her. She was one of the most important people in the palace. That did not matter to her so much as having her opinion asked about every detail that concerned the baby and, best of all, she had a golden pram to push, with a canopy that went up and down and a place for an umbrella. In the palace grounds there were gardens and parks laid out where tame tigers wandered, and already she had had an invitation for her free half day.

After many tearful scenes with Julius, Samantha and Salvatore the film was finished, and the Harper family packed up to go home.

Tiger-nanny promised to spend Christmas with them and a week-end in the Easter holidays and perhaps the summer ones too, so long as the baby prince was doing well and his parents allowed her to go.

Mandoline Harper and her husband left Matsumundu before the children did, having laid the foundation stone for the first cinema of the Matsumundu Group. They would return to open the cinema when it was finished.

The children stayed three weeks longer, until schools had been found for them and the dates of their opening terms were decided. Tiger-nanny privately thought Salvatore was too young to go to boarding-school but he said he wanted to go.

'Why do you want to go, lovey?' she asked him.

'Because I'm a big boy now,' he replied.

'Oh well,' thought Tiger-nanny, 'I have finished my job there and that's what I meant to do.'

But she absentmindedly packed a morsel of his new Fluff in the suitcase, just in case he was homesick when he got to school.

The day came, and they left her. All the tears, and hugs, all the laughter, all the scoldings and fault-

findings were over (they really were very naughty children) and she had the golden kingdom of the royal nursery all to herself. She was queen of her domain and nobody ever again would say they did not want a tiger for a nanny.

Two great tears rolled down Tiger-nanny's nose and splashed upon the floor as she thought of Julius's proud head, Samantha's motherly embraces and Salvatore's misleading innocence. Who would pack for them or unpack when they returned from school? Who would listen to all their adventures when Mandoline was away on location or too busy to bother with them?

Was the royal nursery really a kingdom or just a gilded cage? There were a hundred thousand Matsumunduns ready to care for and worship the little prince, and fifty jealous, trained nurses longing to take her place.

As Tiger-nanny went to air his little nightshirt and nappies for the evening a servant knocked on the door and brought a telegram into the room on a golden plate.

'For me?' said Tiger-nanny in surprise.

She opened it with a hesitating paw and read:

CHILDREN ARRIVED SAFELY. PLEASE, TIGER-NANNY, COME BACK. PLEASE, PLEASE, PLEASE. I REALLY AM HAVING A BABY THIS TIME AND THE DOCTOR SAYS IT'S TWINS.

The signature was *Mandoline Harper*.

Tiger-nanny absently put the nightshirt in her pocket and hung the telegram out to air. Then, faintly at first, but gradually getting louder and louder, she began to purr.